365 Days
of
Affirmations
for a
Year of Bliss

Rochel Marie Lawson, PhD, RN, AHP, CMS

365 Days of Affirmations for a Year of Bliss

Copyright © 2025 Rochel Marie Lawson, PhD, RN, AHP, CMS

ISBN (Paperback): 979-8-89672-093-5
ISBN (Ebook): 979-8-89672-094-2

Printed in the United States of America.

PROMINENT
BOOKS
EDGE

5830 E 2nd St, Ste 7000 #9983
Casper, WY 82609
USA

With gratitude and love, I dedicate this book to my beautiful children, Khrystopher Aaron Lawson and Lauryn Alexis Marie Lawson. Without them, I would not have rediscovered the beauty and power of affirmations or the dynamic process of employing them to take action.

My children reminded me that the power of affirmations is real. It was through Khrystopher and Lauryn that I learned that adding intentions to affirmations lights the fire, energy, and velocity that ultimately turns them into reality.

My children have always inspired and motivated me to take targeted action, to serve others, and to be the best that I can be. They reawakened in me the insight to always know that *I am a queen*!

Contents

Author's Note

This book offers words of wisdom regarding the use of affirmations and intentions and is designed for educational purposes only. You should not rely on this information as a substitute for, nor does it replace professional medical, psychiatric, or business advice, diagnosis, or treatment. If you have concerns or questions about your health, business, or mental well-being, you should always consult with a healthcare or business professional. Do not disregard, avoid, or delay obtaining medical or business-related advice from your healthcare or business professional because of something you may have read here. The use of any information provided in this book is solely at your own risk.

Developments in research may impact the health, business, and life advice that appears here. No assurances can be given that the information contained in this book will always include the most relevant findings or developments with respect to the material.

Having said all that, know that I have shared my wisdom of the utilization of affirmations and intentions with you with a sincere and generous intent to assist you on your journey to living your dream life filled with bliss. Please reach out to me with any questions you may have about the information and use of affirmations and intentions in this book. I will be happy to assist you further!

Introduction

Affirming something without intending to act is just a wish.

Not long ago I took a yearlong journey. This journey entailed me experiencing all aspects of life, the good, the bad, the sad, and the ugly. When I embarked upon this journey, I was in search of something that I could use that would help me get through each day. I was in search of something that was tangible, that I could make my own, that was specific to the needs of my mind, body, and soul, and that fed me with nourishing thoughts and energy as I traveled down my path to bliss.

I was at a point in my life where I was not happy. To others, I looked fabulous. I was on top of the world. I was cute (still am) and physically fit with a figure to die for. I owned a big house, drove luxury cars, had money in the bank, and was a faithful servant in my church.

I owned a successful business. I was on the board of directors for several influential organizations. I was a well-known and highly respected woman in my community.

I had fabulous children who were successful in their own rights and earned accolades in their academic and extracurricular activities.

To others it seemed I had a dream life.

I *did* have a dream life.

But something was missing.

Not only was I not living my dream life, but the life I had been living wasn't even fun.

Can you relate?

Then one day while meditating, I realized I was not feeling whole. I was not feeling complete. I took the time to explore and connect with my innermost thoughts and feelings and realized that something big was missing.

I was going through the motions of living a dream life and being the "have it all gal," but I felt empty. I felt like a fraud. It was in that moment of self-reflection that I became fully aware that I was not, in fact, living my dream life.

Then, as if on cue, chaos ensued and challenges appeared as roadblock on my path to bliss. I faced death in my family, betrayals in business and personal relationships, and negative cash flow. It seemed that almost every aspect of my life was being disrupted.

That's when I decided I needed to look deep within myself to try to find what was missing in my life. I needed to tap into the holistic wisdom and principles I had been studying for more than twenty years and that had helped me so often in the past to find my bliss.

I enjoyed creating and saying affirmations. I had learned to use them when I was a kid running track and field by a famous athlete. This famous athlete shared with me how to use affirmations to motivate myself so that I could achieve the results I desired.

From the moment I learned about affirmations, I would use them to motivate and keep me on track to obtaining what I desired to accomplish. However, the more I believed I was living my dream life, the less and less I participated in my daily practice of affirmations, which was reflected in all aspects of my life.

I've always used affirmations to connect with my true nature and Divine team. The one problem with affirmations is that until you take action, the affirmation is nothing more than a statement of a dream or a wish. To transform affirmations into reality, you must take intentional action.

As the holidays were coming to an end and the challenges in my life surmounted, I decided to go into the new year with a new attitude and a fresh approach to my affirmation practice. I would continue creating and saying my affirmations, but now I would experiment by adding intentions.

This was huge for me because it meant I would not only state an affirmation but I would also challenge myself to take action to turn my affirmation into reality.

As I experimented with this technique, the results were terrific. Each day seemed to get better, and I felt more optimistic. I knew of no one else adding intention to their affirmation, or even talking about it. For some reason, that knowledge fueled my resolve to take my affirmations to a new level. Intention became my superpower, and my superpower would galvanize me to take action to transform my dreams into reality.

Armed with my new superpower, I decided to take a yearlong journey with this new and wild idea of adding intentions to my daily affirmations. I called the phenomenon the A + I Formula: "Affirmation plus Intention." I would apply the A + I Formula to my daily affirmations, then analyze and document the results of how and what I manifested in my life each day and month of that year in my life.

The result blew me away. I not only began understanding the power of the A + I Formula but I also now visualized my dream life with vivid detail. More importantly, I began to live my dream life.

And as they say, the rest is history.

I share this information with you in the hopes that you will use the A + I Formula in your life so you can begin to visualize, create, take divinely-inspired action, and live your dream life as well.

May you enjoy *365 Days of Affirmations for a Year of Bliss* over and over again.

Namaste.

How to Use This Book

I've designed this book to be an easy day-by-day guide that you can use to manifest all that you desire so that you can step into having and living a life of bliss.

Because I want you to experience as much success utilizing what is in this book as I have, I've made it super simple and powerfully effective.

The best way is to start at day 1 and continue until you get to day 365. The beautiful thing about this book is that you can begin using it at any time during the year. All you need to do is start at day 1 and follow the sequence until you reach day 365. Then you can start it all over to continue experiencing years of bliss.

So are you ready to experience a year of bliss?

Here are the steps to follow for maximum results.

- Select your affirmation for the day.
- Take a deep breath in and exhale.
- Read the affirmation silently.
- State the affirmation out loud eight times.
- Take a deep breath in and release it.
- Read the suggested intention.

And most importantly, act each day based on the intention set for that day.

Then start the process again the next day. As you continue to follow the guidelines stated above for using the affirmations and intentions in this book, you will begin to experience profound changes in your wellness, wisdom, and wealth. The process is gradual and continual. This allows the energy to build and the momentum to flow just as it is meant to in your life.

Maintain your deep sense of knowing that everything happens in the quickest, highest, and best way.

The Divine loves action and motion because action creates motion and motion creates energy. The higher the energy, the faster the motion. The more quickly you take intentional action, the faster you will see the results that you desire in your life occur.

The most important thing I would like for you to remember is that if you do not take any action, you will not experience the energy or vibrations that you need to achieve the changes or results that you desire.

It's up to you, however, I don't want you to believe me. I want you to experience the profound fabulousness of bliss for yourself.

You now have a fabulous guide to make having and living a year of bliss so much easier!

Affirmations

Shall we begin?

Day 1

I choose to always honor myself in all that I think and do.

I intend to do something that nurtures my mind and my body such as getting a massage, taking a nature walk, taking a candlelit bath, eating the most nourishing food possible, meditating, exercising, or anything that makes me feel naturally amazing.

Day 2

I know that my energy expands in the world and the more action I take toward my goals, the more the universe will embrace my intention.

I intend to identify a goal and take an action step toward achieving that goal.

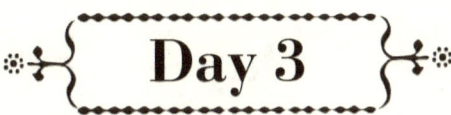

Day 3

I am accepting and loving and becoming more comfortable with my true self.

I intend to spend five minutes in solitude and appreciating myself.

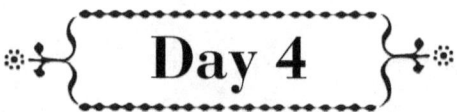

Day 4

I am becoming more comfortable with letting go.
I will let go of the past and release all my fears.
I am *free*!

At the top of each hour, I intend to focus on the beauty of the here and now.

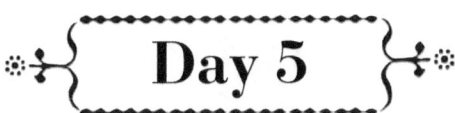

Day 5

I am strong. I am capable. I am unstoppable.

I intend to embrace the confidence and fearlessness that is within me.

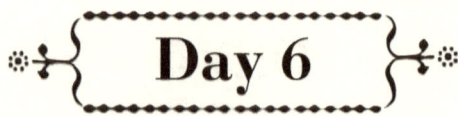

Day 6

I am healthy, radiant, and vibrant.

I intend to eat foods that nourish and satisfy my body and soul.

Day 7

I choose a healthy, nurturing belief system.
I will embrace one day at a time.

I intend to focus on the positive things happening in my life.

Day 8

I am fierce. I am fearless. I am powerful.

I intend to walk with my head held high in a spirit of confidence and grace.

Day 9

I accept love and embrace who I am.

I intend to reflect on the uniquely beautiful being that the Divine created me to be.

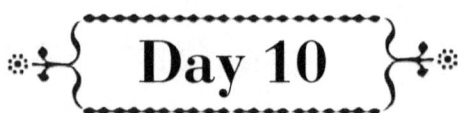

Day 10

I will focus on happiness, harmony, and health.

I intend to take a fifteen-minute walk outdoors, harmonizing with the rhythms of nature.

Day 11

I am tuned in to what is happening in this moment.

I intend to enjoy what is happening right in this moment.

Day 12

I will live my life with a consciousness of love.

I intend to send loving energy to all throughout the world.

Day 13

I will see myself and my life with loving eyes.

I intend to spend a few minutes looking at myself in the mirror today and admiring the loving eyes looking back at me.

Day 14

I am relaxed.

I intend to meditate today.

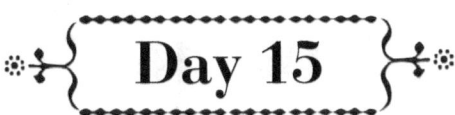

Day 15

I am resourceful.

I intend to cherish the fact that I am clever and identify resourceful ways to swiftly overcome difficulties.

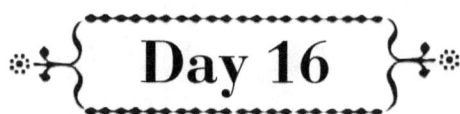

Day 16

I am happy and hopeful.

I intend to smile at every stranger I encounter today.

Day 17

I live with joyous gratitude and appreciation of my life.

Before I go to sleep tonight, I intend to write in my journal about all I am grateful for.

Day 18

I am creative and resilient.

I intend to recognize my ability to gracefully move with the ebb and flow of life.

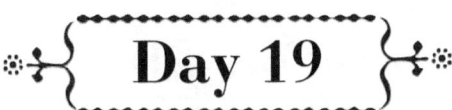

Day 19

I am open to receive all the abundance the universe offers.

I intend to spend a few moments imagining what it would feel like to have my dreams come true.

Day 20

I am determined, peaceful, and relaxed.

I intend to enjoy a day of leisure and freedom from technology.

Day 21

I remain determined, focused, and receptive.

I intend to take a specific, measurable, and laser-focused step toward my goals.

Day 22

My life is flowing with the abundance of joy, peace, and success the universe has bestowed upon me.

I intend to be aware of all the joy, peace, and success I am experiencing.

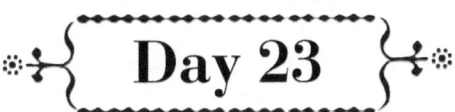

Day 23

I am grateful for the endless blessings that flow into my life. I intend to pay my blessings forward.

Day 24

I am blessed with Divine love.

I intend to spend the day spreading love.

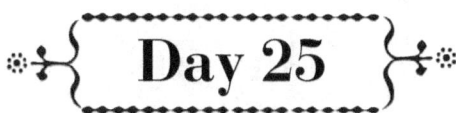

Day 25

I am receptive to the wisdom that is bestowed upon me.

I intend to explore the divinity of the wisdom being bestowed upon me.

Day 26

I will focus on joy, love, and peace.

I intend to focus my thoughts on the aspects of my life that fill me with the emotions of joy, love, and peace.

Day 27

I love my body.

I intend to show my body love with a relaxing massage, a walk in nature, or by taking a warm relaxing bath in candlelight.

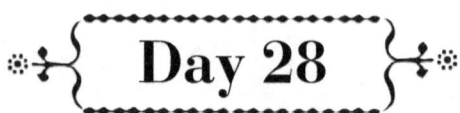

Day 28

My mind is clear and free.

I intend to allow the thoughts of my mind to ebb and flow like the waves of the ocean.

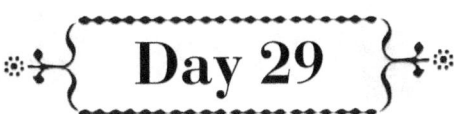

Day 29

My body is energetic, healthy, and well.

I intend to fuel my body with only healthy and nourishing foods.

Day 30

I believe in myself.

I intend to think about all that I have accomplished in my life.

Day 31

I release all worry and live in trust.

I intend to concentrate on the here and now.

Day 32

I have the power to make my dreams a reality.

I intend to embrace the strength within me and revel in the moment.

Day 33

I believe in my ability to create a happy and successful life.

I intend to remember all the happy moments I've experienced in my life and smile at each thought.

Day 34

I cultivate an attitude of success in everything I do.

I intend to walk with confidence as I proceed on my path to bliss.

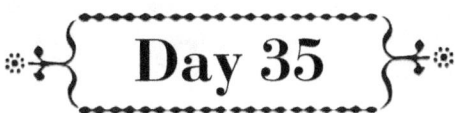

Day 35

I will have trust and keep going.

I intend to thank the Divine for my journey and continue to walk with unshakeable faith.

Day 36

No matter what it takes, I am willing to persevere.

I intend to have a "never give up" attitude as I continue toward my goal.

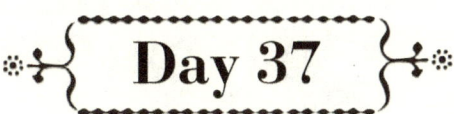

Day 37

I see abundance in every area of my life.

I intend to recognize and be grateful for all the abundance in my life.

Day 38

Every moment of my life is joyous, special, and unique.

I intend to acknowledge the beauty of the uniqueness and special qualities of my life.

Day 39

My mind is clear and receptive.

I intend to mediate for five minutes focusing on the beauty of a clear blue sky.

Day 40

I am free from all illness and disease. My body feels energetic, healthy, and radiant.

I intend to spend time outdoors allowing the rays of the sun to invigorate and nourish my body.

Day 41

My body is burning and dissolving fat at an efficient and noticeable rate.

I intend to take a fifteen-minute walk in nature.

Day 42

I use my time and energy to create the greatest results.

I intend to prioritize my day by completing my most pressing tasks.

Day 43

My thoughts create my reality. I focus on what I always want at all times.

I intend to keep my thoughts positive as I take action on creating the life of my dreams.

Day 44

I accept myself. I accept others. I acknowledge the Divine light within us all.

I intend to send love to all I encounter during this day.

Day 45

I lead a balanced and happy life. I choose harmony.

I intend to dance to my favorite music and sing at the top of my lungs.

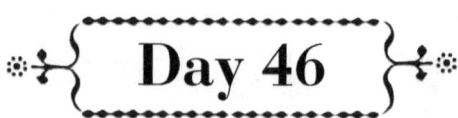

Day 46

I am always surrounded by positive energy.

I intend to express gratitude for the positive energy in my life.

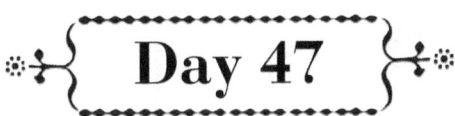

Day 47

I have a positive mental attitude. No matter what is going on, in, or around me, my mental attitude is and stays positive.

I intend to identify all the positive energy flowing around me now.

Day 48

I am valuable and worthy of all the love and blessings I receive.

I intend to embrace my value. I know I am worth more than any amount of gold. I acknowledge that love and blessings flow to me in endless abundance.

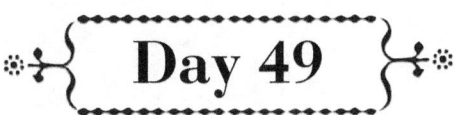

Day 49

I have abundance in every area of my life.

I intend to remove any obstructions from my life that block the flow of abundance.

Day 50

Every moment of my life is special. Joyous appreciation is my constant companion.

I intend to spend this day in gratitude for the joy that I am experiencing right now.

Day 51

I am happy. I am healthy. I am harmonious.

I intend to focus on thoughts that fill me with happiness, health, and harmony.

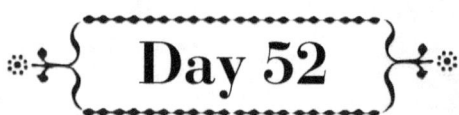

Day 52

I feel healthy and strong. My body feels radiant and vibrant.

I intend to spend twenty minutes walking outdoors in nature while enjoying the warmth and energy of the sun's rays on my skin.

Day 53

I am grateful for the fresh air I breathe, the sun's warmth on my face, and the birdsong in my ears.

I intend to spend twenty minutes enjoying the beauty, gift, and wisdom of nature.

Day 54

I relax and live in peace, patience, and a calm persistence.

I intend to meditate for ten minutes today, focusing on relaxation, peace, and serenity.

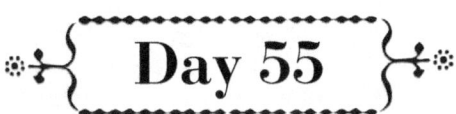

Day 55

My life is filled with love.

I intend to see all the love in my life.

Day 56

I am flexible and open to new ideas.

I intend to be open to receiving the Divine guidance flowing into my life.

Day 57

I am conscious of my resourcefulness, my creativity, and my power to chart a great journey.

I intend to be grateful for the resourcefulness and creativity I experience every day.

Day 58

I am a lucky person. Good things happen to me.

I intend to observe and express gratitude for the goodness flowing to me now.

Day 59

Everything I do adds beauty, harmony, order, and light to the universe.

I intend to spend time picking up trash in my neighborhood, community, or city.

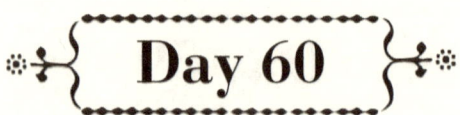

Day 60

I speak positive and uplifting words to honor and serve the greater good of humanity.

I intend to greet all that I meet today with positive and uplifting words.

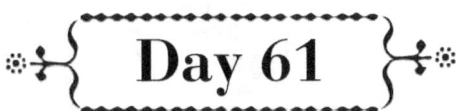

Day 61

I walk and move at a comfortable pace. I do everything at a leisurely tempo. I am relaxed, calm, and tranquil.

I intend to slow down my movements, intentionally take deep breaths, and pay attention to the calmness within me. When I feel myself moving from a state of tranquility and relaxation, I breathe deeply and feel the rush of relaxation flood my body.

Day 62

I visualize myself as a confident, happy, radiant, peaceful, prosperous, and successful person.

I intend to embrace the confident, happy, radiant, peaceful, prosperous, and successful person that I am.

Day 63

I expect the best in my life today and in the future as I always anticipate excellence.

I intend to strive for excellence in all that I do.

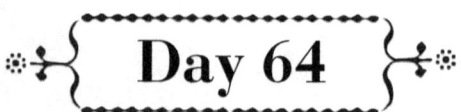

Day 64

I live in an aware and conscious state; I purposely choose the thoughts and images that form a great reality.

I intend to study the beauty of the thoughts and images I have created.

 **Day 65**

I will contemplate my higher self and desire to strengthen the connection. I intend to faithfully ask for a stronger connection to my higher self.

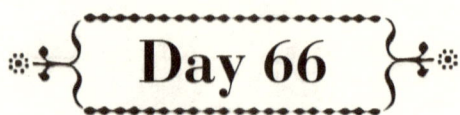

Day 66

I have the power to make this the best day of my life, and I choose to do so.

I intend to be very intentional with my day, only choosing and doing the things that support me in living my best life.

Day 67

I love my body.

I intend to spend time gazing at my body in the mirror and giving thanks to every part, starting with my feet and working my way up to my head. I appreciate and love each unique bone, limb, and organ and thank each for all they do for me.

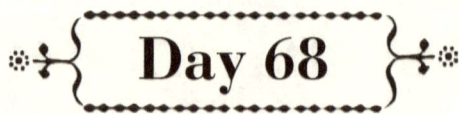

Day 68

I feel healthier and stronger every day.

I intend to visualize the food I intake creating structures of strength and power within me.

Day 69

My body feels amazing.

I intend to love my body by getting a relaxing massage, taking a nice long bath, or a warm steamy shower and thanking the Divine for the gift of having this amazingly beautiful, strong, and powerful body.

Day 70

I chose to live free of envy, fear, judgment, and worry today and every day.

I intend immediately to redirect my musings to generosity, courage, wisdom, and freedom when they become clouded with envy, fear, judgement, and worry.

Day 71

I send my love to all I see and encounter today.

I intend to look in to the mirror and say I love you to the person looking back at me. I will start by whispering the words, and then I'll say them louder and louder and louder until I am bubbling over with love for that person in the mirror. Then I will take all that loving energy with me as I go about my day, spreading it to all I encounter regardless of the specific interactions.

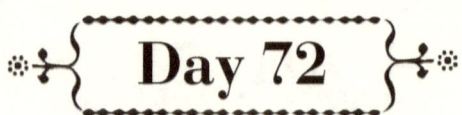

Day 72

I live in alignment with my goal.

I intend to monitor myself throughout the day to make sure I am staying centered and focused. When I discover that I am out of alignment, I will recenter myself by deeply inhaling and exhaling five times to recenter and refocus myself.

Day 73

I lift the veil of illusion. I can see clearly now.

I intend to use today to take what I see at face value. I will not put any meaning into anything that happens in my day. I will just let what happens be the energy of that moment in time and release it back into the universe. I will not internalize it. I will watch and observe as if I'm seeing for the first time.

Day 74

I will take time to treasure the virtue of being in the present moment and appreciate all that I see.

I intend to see each moment just as it presents to me. I will not interpret any meaning into the moment. As I go through my day, I will allow myself to be filled with gratitude for the ability to be present in each moment.

Day 75

I set a reasonable goal every day and hold myself accountable to accomplishing that goal.

I intend to start the day by creating three specific and measurable goals that I will accomplish today. I will also create three specific action steps for each goal to ensure I remain steadfast in my resolve to accomplish the stated goals. I intend to complete each goal before moving to the next.

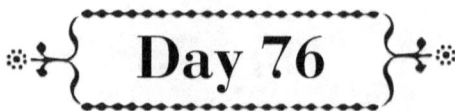

Day 76

I am open to the clarity, grace, power, and wisdom of my own spirit.

I intend to start my day with ten minutes of meditation, during which I will hone in on the words clarity, grace, power, and wisdom. I will silently chant these words as I meditate and allow their power to inhabit my mind, body, and soul.

Day 77

I am calm, peaceful, and positive. I send this energy out to all that I encounter, see, meet, or speak with.

I intend to set my mind and actions to positivity. I will repeat the words calm, peaceful, and positive twenty times while I dress and prepare for my day. I will allow the power of these words to fill and energize my entire being.

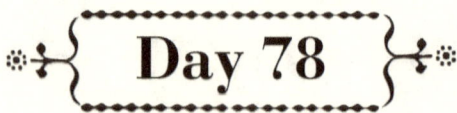

Day 78

I know. I believe. I can.

I intend to accept the fact that I know who I am, that I believe I can do anything, and that I can be the best in the world at whatever I choose to do with my life.

Day 79

I am a kind, loving, and positive person. I embrace this with my mind, body, and soul.

I intend to absorb the energy of my kind, loving, and positive personality and share this part of me with everyone I encounter on my path today. I will revel in the fact that I am the person I am meant to be and will share myself with the world.

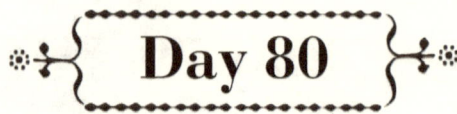

Day 80

I love to laugh. It is healthy, healing, joyful, energizing, and releasing. I am laughing now.

I intend to do an eight-minute laughing meditation to start my day. I will set the timer for eight minutes. I will sit in my favorite place and think of something funny and start laughing out loud, and if I can't think of anything funny, I will just fake laughing until it turns into real laughter.

Day 81

I release all fear and doubt. I open myself to the energy of confidence, fierceness, love, and success.

I intend to do something that I have never done, such as public speaking, being a guest on a podcast, writing something vulnerable, or sharing myself with the world. I open that part of me that says *yes, I can do anything*!

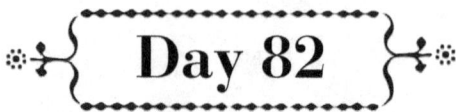

I broadcast to the universe that I am healthy, happy, and elated and revel in joy as the universe returns it to me in abundance.

I intend to bless all I encounter with my exuberant energy. I send blessings of joy to all and open my heart to receive the goodness of happiness and well-being that is shared with me in return.

Day 83

I visualize my day filled with light and positive energy. All that I do today is a success.

I intend to hone in on my positive thoughts, energy, vibrations, and frequencies. Anything that does not warm my heart and soul I will release to keep a clear, open space for the energy of positivity to flow to me.

Day 84

My mind is healthy and filled with all the harmonizing energy I need to get me through my day with clarity and peace of mind.

I intend to open my mind and allow the harmonizing energy from the Divine to penetrate every cell in my brain as it creates the ultimate balance within my mind as I go through my day.

Day 85

I am prosperous and giving. A financial blessing is flowing in my life now.

I intend to clean out all the items I no longer need or use and donate them to people in need or a charitable organization. As I release the items, I infuse them with blessings for those who may receive them.

Day 86

I am in harmony with the universe. Happiness, health, and peace fill my mind and body now.

I intend to be in harmony with the energy of the universe and allow into my life the positive energy of happiness, well-being, and peace. I allow this energy to fill my mind and my body throughout the day.

Day 87

I am a good person.

I intend to welcome the fact that I am a good person with good intentions for myself and the world I live in. I send beautiful and enhancing energy to all I meet today.

Day 88

I am a money magnet. I attract prosperity into my life easily and successfully.

I intend to express gratitude for the prosperity flowing into my life by giving the gift of prosperity to someone else. I may decide to buy a homeless person a meal, pay for the person's coffee behind me in line, donate unused clothing, or donate my time in my community. My goal is to be grateful for my blessings and enjoy the energy of passing on a bit of prosperity to someone else.

Day 89

Divine guidance leads and guides me in all my ways. Perfect health and well-being are mine. The principles of right action guide my life.

I intend to spend time expressing gratitude for the blessings that I have and that are flowing into my life. I give thanks for all the Divine wisdom that has guided me on my journey. I appreciate the gift of well-being.

Day 90

I am grateful for this moment right now, for the previous moment, and for the next moment. I am grateful for all the moments of my life.

I intend to spend one minute of each hour giving thanks and filling my heart with gratitude for the blessings that I receive each moment of every day. During these single moments of gratitude, I fill my heart with the light of love.

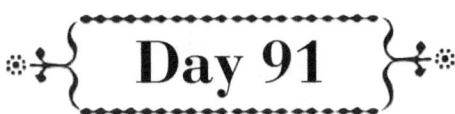

Day 91

I have a beautiful body and a smart mind. I make wise decisions that are in line with my Divine and true nature.

I intend to look at my naked beautiful body in the mirror and rest assured that there is no other body on the planet with the same beauty. My mind is smart, and I make the right decisions by utilizing the gift of my true nature.

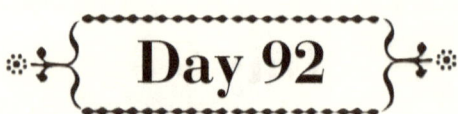

Day 92

The light of my soul guides me. All the answers I seek are coming to me now, and I open my mind to receive this Divine wisdom.

I intend to spend fifteen minutes in quiet solitude. I will seek Divine guidance on the answers that escape me. I allow this time to open the space creating a conduit for me to hear and understand the wisdom from the Divine.

Day 93

I am tranquil and serene. I attract goodness into my life.

I intend to spend time in nature without any agenda other than appreciating the beauty and tranquility of nature. When I appreciate the natural beauty around me, I am able to maintain a state of balance and harmony.

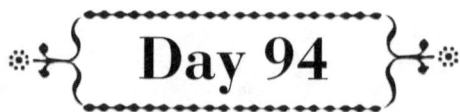

Day 94

I nourish my body with good food, lots of movement, and time in nature. I embrace the restorative qualities this brings to my essence.

I intend to eat organic, non-GMO, pesticide-, and hormone-free foods with each meal. After each meal, I will take a ten-minute walk outside in nature appreciating all the natural and healthy energy I just fueled my body with.

Day 95

My body is relaxed and at ease. I embrace the healthy energy and the positive vibrations of the universe. My body falls in rhythm with the way of the world.

I intend to pamper my body with a treat to keep my body balanced, f lowing, energized, and radiant. The treat might entail a yummy, healthy smoothie, a massage, a bath, or maybe a nice swim. Whatever I decide to do, the goal is to let my body feel how much I appreciate the healthy relaxed energy that it provides to me each day.

Day 96

I imagine a life of gratitude, health, love, peace, and joy. I imagine, and everything that I imagine and visualize is becoming reality.

I intend to keep my thoughts focused on the positivity flowing into my life. I harness that energy of positivity and allow it to feed my soul. As I take in this spiritual nourishment, I know that I am fueling my here and now for the beauty, love, and joy of my future.

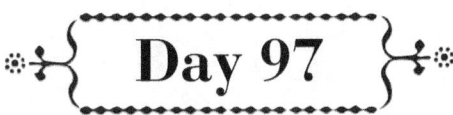

Day 97

I am tranquil and serene. I attract good people, situations, and opportunities into my life.

I intend to spend the day by a body of water such as a creek, lake, river, pond, ocean, or swimming pool. I will take time to gaze into the water and see the reflection of the sky. This is my anchor. Life is amazing and possibilities are limitless.

Day 98

I release all worry from my mind and live in a reality of faith and trust. I have the power to make my dream life a reality.

I intend to have undeniable belief in myself and my ability to take action to live the life of my dreams. I know when I add faith and trust, I set in motion what I desire to become my reality.

Day 99

I release impatience. I foster an attitude of anticipation and excitement. What I want in life flows to me now.

I intend to practice a laughing meditation where I spend five minutes laughing as hard as I can even if I have nothing to laugh about. If necessary, I will fake laugh. I know that by the end of this meditation, I will release real heartfelt pearls of laughter that will fill my spirit as it receives the myriad blessings from the Divine.

Day 100

I change all the negative vibrations that enter my mind into positive vibrations by focusing on the things that I love. Every time a negative thought comes into my mind, I think of the word love.

I intend to write the word love eight times each hour during the next four hours if I have a negative thought and four times each hour during the next four hours if I have no negative thoughts. Each time I write the word love, I will say it out loud and know I am raising the positive energetic vibrations within and around me.

Day 101

I am kind, caring, confident, capable, and successful. I decide what I want in life, and I go after it determined and unafraid.

I intend to take three action steps toward accomplishing something that I have been longing to do. The first step I will take will be the catalyst for the next two. The second step will be the fuel that ignites the fire within me to just *do it*! The third action step will be the step that sees me successfully completing the action I set out to complete today.

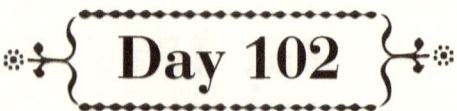

Day 102

I visualize myself standing in my power pose and exuding confidence, fearlessness, radiance, and strength.

I intend to silently repeat the words power, confidence, fearlessness, radiance and strength, throughout the day allowing the energy and vibrations of the words to fill and surround my body.

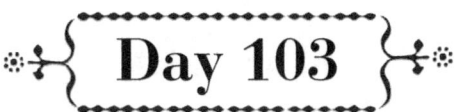

Day 103

Wealth flows to me in abundance and with ease. I know that all I need is being provided to me now, and I am grateful.

I intend to focus my thoughts on the abundance that is flowing into my life and express gratitude to the Divine for the gifts of abundance flowing to me. I know this will open a gateway for more abundance to flow into my life. I am grateful.

Day 104

My heart is filled with love. Therefore, I am loved.

I intend to send loving thoughts to my body, mind, and soul. In addition, I will send loving thoughts to my family, friends, and even those that I do not care for. I will send loving thoughts to the flowers, plants, trees, and birds. I will connect to the emotion of love.

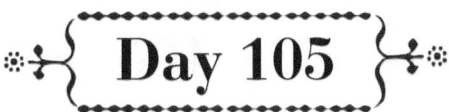

Day 105

All that I want is flowing into my life at this present moment. I have no need to feel lack or deprivation because all that I want is in the palm of my hand.

I intend to donate my unused or seldom-used clothing items to a charitable organization. I intend to focus on the cup being half full instead of half empty. I recognize that I am blessed and do whatever I can to pay it forward.

Day 106

I appreciate what I have in my life right now. I am grateful for all my blessings, and I am honored to be bestowed with the wisdom of this moment.

I intend to spend five minutes in gratitude before I start my daily activities. Every three hours, I will take one minute to focus on the word gratitude and allow the gift of grace to fill my heart.

Day 107

My soul is at peace. Therefore, I am at peace.

I intend to spend time meditating on what the word peace means to me and allow the energy and vibration of the word peace to reside within me. Instead of saying hello as my greeting to those I encounter, today I will say peace.

Day 108

I am open to messages I receive from the universe.

I intend to pay attention to the subtle and not so subtle messages from the universe. I will take note of the theme of the messages and know that I am being divinely guided on this part of my journey.

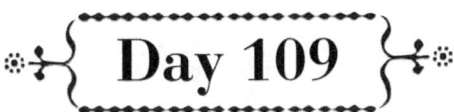

Day 109

I live with passion and personal power. I make my own decisions and act on my own behalf. The choices I make are for me and are in my best interest.

I intend to focus on me, my passion, my personal power, and what I want to do in life. I will make myself the number one priority, and I will not be apologetic for doing so.

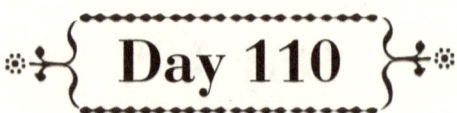

Day 110

I seek the good in all that I do. I look for win-win situations in all my endeavors.

I intend to honor the goodness within me. I see options that are beneficial to all involved.

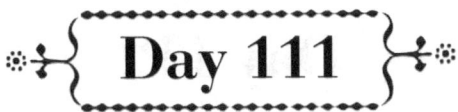

Day 111

I am an enlightened being. My spirit is filled with wisdom, and my soul radiates the light of the Divine.

I intend to honor the gift of light that the Divine provides me by sharing that gift with all I encounter. I know that by doing this, the best version of me will show up no matter what occurs in my day.

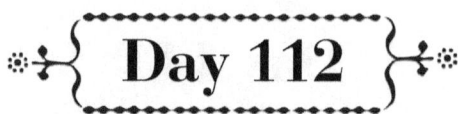

Day 112

I see and focus on all the beauty in the world. I am surrounded by beauty.

I intend to see only the beauty that exists in the world. I will start with myself and move to seeing the beauty in others, the beauty in nature.

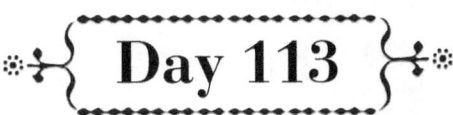

Day 113

Prosperity flows to me in avalanches of abundance.

I intend to imagine the ocean of prosperity's waves flowing into my life, filling all the buckets in my life, allowing me to be debt free. I am a magnet for the ocean of prosperity's waves. I feel the waves beginning to brush the shore of my life.

Day 114

Day by day, in every way, I am becoming more and more successful. I incorporate the wisdom of my experiences in life and use this to become better and better at what I do.

I intend to spend time acknowledging the successes I've experienced in my life up until now. I take the energy of those successes and allow it to fuel my soul, knowing that things are only going to get better.

Day 115

I stop and take a moment to realize when I have fallen into a less active pathway. I observe it without holding on to it, and then I let it go, choosing a more suitable option.

I intend to accept the fact that I have less active pathways that prevent me from being the best that I can be. I acknowledge that I am not my less active pathway and use it as a guide to get back on track in a positive manner.

Day 116

I wake up feeling energized, rested, and rejuvenated every day.

I intend use my energized state to do a household chore that I have been neglecting such as gardening, cleaning out the garage, clearing out the attic, pruning the trees, or cleaning the gutters. Expending energy in this manner is good for balancing my body and mind.

Day 117

I go to sleep with a mind that is at peace, relaxed, and ready for slumber.

I intend to refrain from using any electronics at least one hour prior to my bedtime. When I get in my bed, I release all thoughts of the day and focus on my breathing to induce a deep, restful, and peaceful sleep.

Day 118

My mind is open, clear, and ready to receive the solutions I seek.

I intend to get quiet and pay attention to the subtle and the overt messages that the Divine is sending me. I know these messages contain the answers I seek. With an open and clear mind, the solutions I desire are revealed.

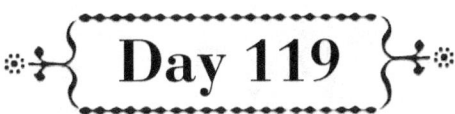

Day 119

My bedroom is the perfect place for a good night's slumber. It is calming, relaxing, and restorative. When I lay in my bed, I fall fast asleep.

I intend to prepare my bedroom for sleep by closing the curtains or blinds, turning off all lights, and spraying my pillow with the calming and relaxing scent of lavender.

Day 120

I trust in the wisdom of my subconscious mind. It is always working for my highest good.

I intend to spend five minutes journaling about what I believe my subconscious mind is telling me. I will allow the pen to flow freely on the pages of the journal as my subconscious mind reveals to me what it wants me to know at this moment in time.

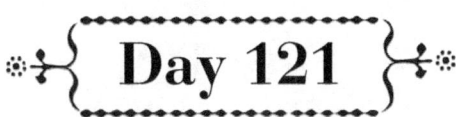

Day 121

I allow my subconscious mind to roam freely while I sleep so I will awaken with the answers I seek.

I intend to fall asleep listening to soothing music designed to allow me to drift off to slumber with ease. As I drift off to sleep, my conscious mind takes a rest and my subconscious mind becomes active.

Day 122

I surrender my mind to positive thoughts.

I intend to focus on only positive thoughts, knowing that the more I do this, the more positive my energy and vibrations will be.

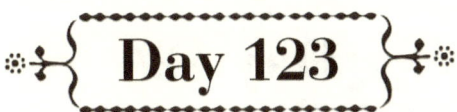

Day 123

I focus on providing my body with the best nourishment I can afford. This helps to strengthen my immune system and keep me feeling healthy, strong, and vibrant.

I intend to make a green smoothie with kale, spinach, apples, pears, and water. This will enhance my health and give a boost to my immune system.

Day 124

My body functions at an optimal level, my mind is clear and calm, and my imagination is vivid and free.

I intend to spend fifteen minutes in silent gratitude for all that my body does automatically that allows me to feel healthy, vibrant, and full of energy. During this time in silent gratitude, I imagine all that I dream about becoming a reality.

Day 125

My digestive system is a fat-burning system that allows my metabolism to effectively utilize the food that I take in.

I intend to eat food my *dosha* requires to keep it balanced, healthy, and operating at an optimal level. I know by doing this I provide my digestive system the correct fuel it needs to keep my body operating efficiently.

Day 126

I welcome the clarity, wisdom, grace, and power of my spiritual being.

I intend to create space during my day to be quiet and tap into the wisdom of my intelligent mind. I listen to the guidance and incorporate the wisdom I receive into my life with grace and ease.

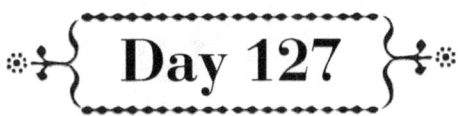

Day 127

I am the mastermind of my life. I visualize and create the life of my dreams.

I intend to spend fifteen minutes visualizing the blueprint for the life I desire to live. I take time to add specific detail to each aspect of my visualization. I know the more detail I add, the more I can see it as my reality.

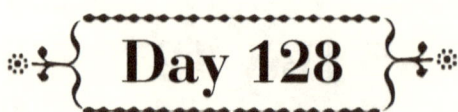

Day 128

I am prosperous in all my ways. I accept the generosity of the Divine universe.

I intend to have thoughts of prosperity and abundance flowing into my life. I envision the gateway to prosperity opening in my life as wide as the Pacific Ocean, and I am filled with gratitude.

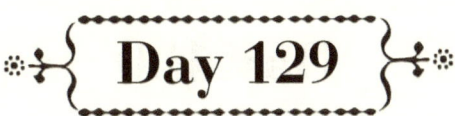

Day 129

My investments are protected, and my wealth is growing every day.

I intend to invest 10 percent of my monthly income in a stock or investment of my choice. I choose investments that represent what I value and that offer the best return for my investment.

Day 130

I create my reality each day, and today's reality: I am a success in all that I do.

I intend to recognize and appreciate all the successes I have experienced in the last thirty days. I am filled with gratitude for my accomplishments and now thank the Divine for the gift of perseverance.

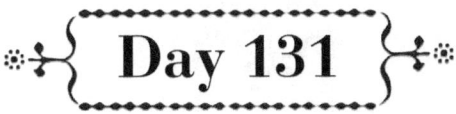

Day 131

I have a healthy and radiant body. I am filled with healthy and radiant energy. I am healthy and radiant.

I share my healthy and radiant energy with all I encounter. I know that sharing healthy and radiant energy with others allows me to replenish my supply of healthy and radiant energy as well.

Day 132

It is safe for me to follow my path to bliss. I unlock spiritual resources that assist with keeping my path free from challenges. I am divinely protected as I travel on my path to bliss.

I intend to tap into the orgasmic energy of bliss. I allow this energy to fill and invigorate my soul, and with this, I flow throughout my day in a state of ecstasy.

Day 133

I am free from debt and wealth flows to me in showers of abundance.

I intend to spend five minutes each hour of the day visualizing a shower of the abundance I desire flowing into my life. As I visualize this beautiful shower of abundance, I see my debt flowing away and my river and reservoir of prosperity growing.

Day 134

I exist as an island of peace and calm even when I am in a sea of ambiguity.

I intend to practice being in a peaceful state by visualizing I am as calm and peaceful as the blue and tranquil sea or serene lake on a beautiful spring day. I am the peace within this vision.

Day 135

Even when my world is immersed in darkness, I walk forward in faith, love, peace, and light.

I intend to share my beautiful bright light of love with the universe.

Day 136

I am optimistic about the healthy changes that I am making in all aspects of my life.

I intend to see this journey with my health and well-being as something that is fun, wholesome, relaxing, healing, energizing, and loving. I know small changes lead to big results.

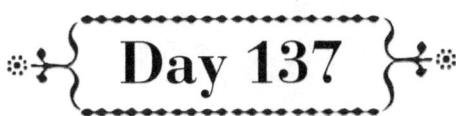

Day 137

My body is functioning right now at an optimal level. As I go through the day, my body synchronizes, harmonizes, and operates efficiently.

I intend to take a nice long shower or bath and allow the warm water to soothe my body as it cleans and detoxifies me. I know that this, too, allows my body to flow in a more harmonic and natural state. And I am grateful.

Day 138

In this moment, I am free.

I intend to enjoy this moment for what it is without any expectation of what I think it should be. This is my moment.

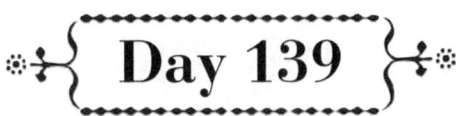

Day 139

I am in touch with my emotional guidance system as it holds the keys to how I am living in the present moment.

I intend to pay attention to the information that my emotional guidance system is sharing with me right now. I know that this information is valuable and will not ever lead me astray from what is in my best and highest good.

Day 140

I am blessed. Good things are happening in my life, and I am grateful.

I intend to spend three minutes out of each hour to think of all I have to be grateful for. I know when I ponder that which I am grateful for, I send out positive and loving energy into the universe, which magnetizes more blessings to me.

Day 141

I am positive and peaceful. I am surrounded by positive and peaceful energy and vibrations.

I intend to spend a few moments in nature listening to the birds sing, looking at the blossoming flowers and trees, and feeling the earth beneath my feet. I allow the energy and vibrations of nature to fill my body with peace.

Day 142

I am filled with kindness and compassion. I am loved, and I give love.

I intend to greet everyone I encounter with smiling eyes and a smiling face. This will allow me to generate vibrations of love and kindness and open my heart chakra to feel more compassion toward all living things.

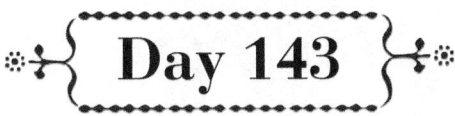

Day 143

I have a strong and healthy mind. I am wise. I use my wisdom for the betterment of my life.

I intend to raise the vibrations in my mind by focusing on all the positive aspects of my life. As I do this, I know that my mind is being energized with positive, loving, and healing light. This allows the opening of the doorway to Divine wisdom to expand and grow.

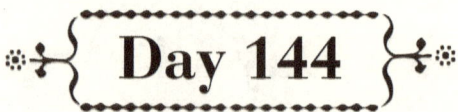

Day 144

I trust the inner messages that I receive. They lead me to make the right decision at the right time.

I intend to meditate in a quiet place to open my third eye chakra, which will deepen my connection to the universe and strengthen my mental clarity so I know I am making the right decisions.

Day 145

I respect my ability to be creative, kind, and giving. This is my true nature, and I embrace it today and every day moving forward.

I intend to repeat this affirmation three times at the top of every hour for the next three hours. I allow the vibrations of the words of this affirmation to flow within my body, starting with the top of my head and flowing down to the bottom of my feet. This will keep my creative, kind, and giving vibrations humming throughout the day.

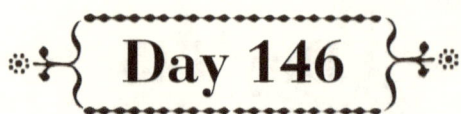

Day 146

I consciously choose thoughts that create trust, harmony, positivity, and peace of mind. This helps to keep me balanced.

I intend to choose my thoughts carefully with the goal of focusing on trust, harmony, positivity, and peace of mind and what these words mean to me. As I do this, I become aware of how balancing and uplifting each of these words are, and this brings peace to my soul.

Day 147

It is safe for me to follow my passion and turn it into my purpose. I make choices that honor my spirit.

I intend to write down two goals that I want to accomplish that are related to either my passion or my purpose or both. I proceed forward by completing the actions needed to complete my goals.

Day 148

I program my mind to get rid of negative thoughts. I connect to my intuition, which guides me through this process.

I intend to shift each negative thought that enters my mind by writing in my journal two blessings I have received. I know that the guidance that my intuition provides me is always right.

Day 149

I am a powerful creator. I am open-minded and always eager to turn my creations into a reality.

I intend to take action to create something that I've wanted to create for a long time. I know that when I keep my creations in my head, I deprive myself and others from benefitting from their beauty and goodness.

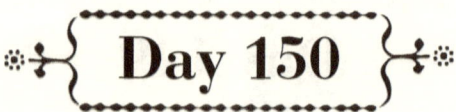

Day 150

I smile because I know I am doing my best, and it makes my heart feel amazing and loved.

I intend to smile at myself every time I pass by a mirror. I use this as a reminder that I am doing the best that I can, I am beautiful, and I am loved.

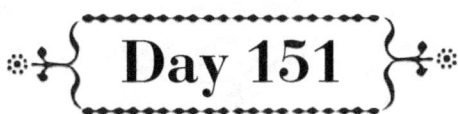

Day 151

I focus on all the good things that my body does for me. I strive to give my body the best nourishment, exercise, and sleep that I possibly can. I know that this aids in keeping my body healthy and well.

I intend to eat lots of leafy green vegetables and fruit, walk for ten to fifteen minutes after eating my biggest meal of the day, and get at least seven hours of sleep tonight.

Day 152

I am grateful for the blessings in my life. The Divine takes care of all my needs.

I intend to turn over all my worries and cares to the Divine. I step out into the world with gratitude and confidence that all my needs are taken care of. As I do this, I free my mind to be open to seeing all the blessings in my life.

Day 153

I am free from the worry of establishing unreasonable schedules and expectations.

I intend to release and let go of my timeline of expectation regarding what I desire in my life. I know that by releasing expectation, I free myself from disappointment and doubt. What I desire is being drawn to me now.

Day 154

I am becoming the person I have always dreamed of. I embrace this as my eternal truth and know that there is true power in embracing this fact.

I intend to release the need to be what others want me to be and step into what I desire myself to be. Releasing the need to satisfy the needs of what others think I should be frees my soul and allows me to express the true me.

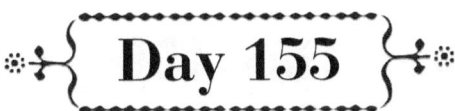

Day 155

I will practice being the kind of person that I would want to love. I open my heart chakra to fill it with the energy of the color pink, the color of love. I allow this pink light and energy to completely fill my entire body.

I intend to act in a loving manner with all that I interact with no matter what the circumstance or situation may be. I send the loving energy and light of the color of pink to all I encounter, and it feels amazing.

Day 156

I release the past, enjoy the present, and move into the future with joy and excitement.

I intend to enjoy the blessings I have and look forward to the future. Doing this allows me to appreciate all that I have now and to eagerly and excitedly look forward to the future.

Day 157

I am free.

I intend to spend eight minutes journaling about what being free means to me at this moment in my life. I can use this as a reminder when I feel overwhelmed by the challenges of my life.

Day 158

I am Successful.

I intend to spend fifteen minutes thinking about and acknowledging all the success I've had in my life. When my mind begins to wander away from the thoughts of my success, I lovingly guide it back to focusing on all my successes.

Day 159

I will surprise anyone who underestimates me.

I intend to exhibit the energy of being fearless. For it is within the energy of being fearless that I can be in total command of my life.

Day 160

I am receptive to the wisdom being bestowed upon me. I embrace this wisdom and incorporate it into my life.

I intend to spend time in quiet and solitude so that I can listen to the wisdom and guidance that I am now receiving. This is not only soothing to my soul but it also becomes easier to hear the wisdom I am receiving.

Day 161

I know that actions speak louder than words.

I intend to pay attention to the action of those around me. I look to see if their actions match up to their words. If there is a disconnect with their actions and words, I know that I should release them from my life.

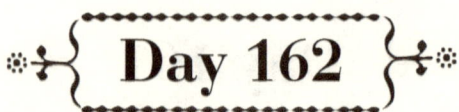

Day 162

I am living in the present moment. I am focused on the here and now. When my thoughts begin to wander, I return my focus back to the here and now. The present moment.

I intend to focus on the present moment—the here and now—right now. I will do this all day to keep myself grounded and free. Focusing on the present moment allows me to enjoyit, which is a gift from the Divine.

Day 163

I am a trendsetter. I am a leader. I am creative.

I intend to claim and own the trendsetter that I am as a brave, bold, and unstoppable leader by exhibiting that aspect of me in all that I do. I know that it is safe for me to be the trendsetting, creative leader that I am. I make no apologies.

Day 164

I have a creative mind. I focus on allowing my imagination to be as creative as it can be in all that I do. It is OK and safe for me to think outside the box.

I intend to remove limitations and give permission for my creative mind to be free.

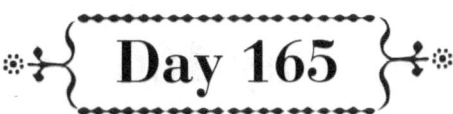

Day 165

I am in touch with my internal guidance system. I feel its vibration and know that it is all-wise and guiding me to make the best decision at this moment in time.

I intend to pay attention to the feelings in my gut when I make a decision. I allow the feelings in my gut to guide me to make the correct decision. I trust my "gut feelings." They never lead me astray.

Day 166

My words are powerful. I choose to use them wisely.

I intend to speak loving words to myself. I value the power of my words, especially when I use them on myself. Doing this opens my throat chakra and allows the vibrations of the loving words to fill my body with loving light.

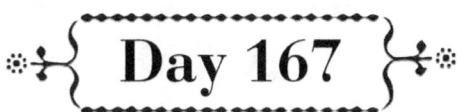

Day 167

I maintain peace in all situations. I am at peace in this present moment. Today my decisions are rooted in peace.

I intend to apply peaceful solutions to all adversarial encounters. Being in a peaceful state is healthy for my mind, body, and soul. I love peace and the way it feels within me.

Day 168

I am practicing the art of surrender. I trust and let go knowing that all is how it is supposed to be.

I intend to release and let go of all that does not feel good to me. As I release and let go, I open space for peace to flow into me.

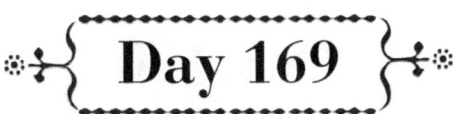

Day 169

Serenity is all around me, prosperity is flowing into my life, abundance is being bestowed upon me, and I am open to receive.

I intend to spend time in nature enjoying the peace that exists there. I know that nature is continually filled with abundance and serenity, and this is where I want to be. Doing this opens space for me to receive more abundance in my life.

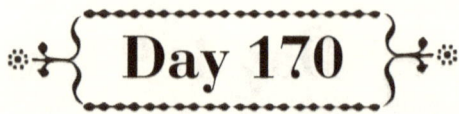

Day 170

I am worthy of love. When I love myself, I expand and open my heart to give and receive love.

I intend to spend time looking at myself in the mirror, telling myself how much I love the other person looking back at me. Saying I love myself while looking in the mirror is one of the most loving things that I can do for myself. I understand that it is OK for me to love myself.

Day 171

My thoughts create my reality. I choose my thoughts carefully and charge them with positive energy.

I intend to be mindful of the words I use when speaking to myself and to others. I use words that are uplifting and motivating, positive and happy, empowering and healing, and enduring and strong.

Day 172

I am practicing the art of self-love. I love myself. I love my mind. I love my body. I love my spirit. I love who I am.

I intend to spend time loving my mind, body, and spirit by taking a walk in nature or doing something that brings a smile to my face and joy to my heart, such as playing with my dog or taking a long, warm, soothing bath with candles and relaxing and calming essential oils.

Day 173

I am powerful.

I intend to make all decisions from a position of power and strength. Knowing that when I do this, I honor myself, my integrity, my mind, my body, and my soul.

Day 174

Serenity is all around me, prosperity is f lowing into my life, and abundance is being given to me. I am open to receive all that the Divine is sending to me now.

I intend to allow myself to welcome the serenity that is in my life, knowing that by doing this, I am magnetizing more of what I desire in my life. This is the conduit that opens me up to the gift of receiving all that is rightfully mine.

Day 175

I know that the universe is expansive and abundant. All that I desire is available to me.

I intend to take time to record all that I desire, recognize how it is flowing into my life, and give thanks to the abundant universe for the blessings it is continuously delivering to me.

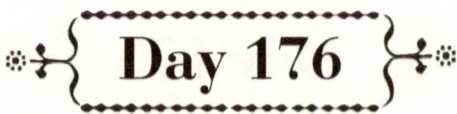

Day 176

I feel good. I feel positive. I let go of my ego, and I relax into the flow of my life.

I intend to allow the good energy and positive vibrations of the universe to fill my mind and my body. This will be the nectar that feeds my soul and guides me on my path to bliss.

Day 177

Each thought brings me a sense of clarity, a new idea, and an open insight.

I intend to let my mind run wild with thoughts of pleasure, happiness, joy, and peace, knowing that this will open a gateway to the unlimited resources.

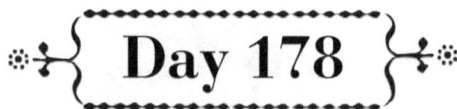

Day 178

A journey is meant to be experienced. My journey is a one-of-a-kind experience and is unique to me. No other person will have the same journey as me, and that is amazing, which means that I am amazing.

I intend to relish in the fact that I am unique, amazing, and beautiful.

Day 179

I am free of all debt, and prosperity flows to me and is all around me. I recognize all the prosperity in my life, and I am grateful.

I intend to spend fifteen minutes gathering all the material possessions that I no longer need and then donating them to a charitable organization such as Good Will, women veterans organizations, or a homeless shelter so that they may assist those in need.

Day 180

I am free from all pain and suffering. The energy of health and well-being is flowing into my body, and I am grateful.

I intend to do something for my body that brings me joy, peace, and relaxation. Such as getting a spa treatment, massage, or taking a Pilates class. I understand that this is a fabulous way to say thank you to my body for all that it provides to me.

Day 181

I am always at the right place at the right time.

I intend to pay attention to all that happens in my life and know that nothing happens by chance. All that happens in my life is part of my Divine journey.

Day 182

I chose to spend quality time with people that I love.

I intend to tell everyone I love how much they mean to me and how I am blessed to have them in my life. I know that by doing this, I am honoring myself, those that I love and care about, and the Divine creator.

Day 183

I have all the wisdom I need to make today a great day.

I intend to take action that honors and realigns my soul. I recognize when I am out of alignment. I value the gift of the wisdom being bestowed upon me.

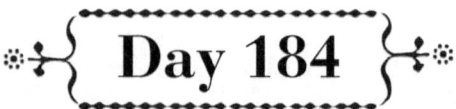

Day 184

I pause throughout the day to recognize the wisdom that is being shared with me. I value this wisdom as I know that it is a Divine gift meant only for me.

I intend to spend a minute out of each hour in gratitude for the wisdom being granted to me now.

Day 185

I am filled with Divine light. This light balances, nourishes, and harmonizes all the functions of my body.

I intend to acknowledge the light within me and share that light with all that I encounter. I know that by doing this, I send my gifts of life to all.

Day 186

I breathe in healthy, harmonizing, and happy energy. I breathe out ill, chaotic, and negative energy.

I intend to think healthy, happy, and harmonizing thoughts, knowing that when I do this, I connect with the life-giving universal energy of life.

Day 187

I am worry and anxiety free. The Divine is handling all my needs. I believe, have faith, and trust that all is perfect and as it should.

I intend to spend twenty minutes journaling about all that is on my mind. I know that by doing this, I open the gateway for all that is safe, comforting, and loving to flow on to the pages of my journal, which is releasing and healing.

Day 188

I claim what is rightfully mine.

I intend to spend time acknowledging what is rightfully mine and accepting all of it whether good, bad, or indifferent. Doing this allows me to place myself in a neutral position of receiving, which is exactly where I desire to be.

Day 189

I am increasing my water intake daily. Today I will drink one more glass of water than I drank yesterday.

I intend to focus on keeping my body hydrated by drinking seven to eight glasses of water. I know this balances, nourishes, hydrates, and detoxifies my body inside and out.

Day 190

I strive to be the best that I can be. I focus on today, and that is all that I focus on. I stay focused and present.

I intend to think before I speak, act with integrity, and not take anything personally. By acting in this capacity, I honor myself and all whom I encounter.

Day 191

I surround myself with peaceful, positive, and prosperous people that are giving, fun, genuine, and loving.

I intend to spend time with people that nourish my soul, that radiate happy and loving energy, and that make me laugh. I choose to spend time playing with the children in my life, playing on a playground, and tapping into the essence of children at play.

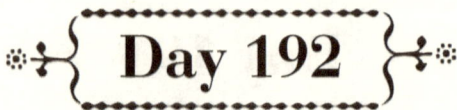

Day 192

I eat food that is nourishing to my body and balancing to my mind. It strengthens my immune system and opens my mind, allowing the release of creativity within me to come to the surface.

I intend to drink a green smoothie, have a salad with a healthy protein, and meditate in silence for fifteen minutes undisturbed. This is harmonizing to the *doshas* of my body and mind.

Day 193

My imagination is unlimited, and my visualizations are vivid. I can create all that I imagine and see. The more detail I add to what I visualize, the more real the visualization becomes, which aids in making my dreams a reality.

As I lay in bed before I drift off to sleep, I imagine one aspect of my dreams, adding as much detail as possible. As I drift off to sleep, I keep the vision of my dreams in my mind and allow it to flow into my infinite intelligent mind where the magic of creation begins.

Day 194

Every second of this day, my life is filled with blessings. The more I take time to recognize the gift of these blessings, the more beautiful my life continues to be. The gift of life is truly a blessing for me.

I intend to spend three minutes in gratitude this morning and five minutes in gratitude this evening. I focus on allowing my heart to be filled with the loving energy of gratitude, and I radiate this energy out into the world.

Day 195

Instead of holding on to what I could have done, I am taking action to do what I can do now.

I intend to release all feelings associated with guilt, doubt, and failure. I release these feelings by focusing on what I can do now. I understand that there are no failures in life. There are only lessons learned. I am in the process learning, growing, and becoming wiser.

Day 196

I am confident in my ability to create my own happiness. I am confident in my ability to bring joy to the world.

I intend to spend the day doing things that make me happy and make my heart sing. I will smile at everyone I see today, and I will send them all lots radiant energy of happiness and joy.

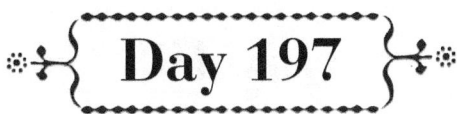

Day 197

I am too busy reinventing myself to worry about past mistakes. I focus on this moment right now, knowing that I am brave enough to be who I truly am.

I intend to spend time looking at myself in the mirror and telling the face looking back at me how confident, courageous, and savvy I am, knowing this is healthy for my mind, spirit, and emotions.

Day 198

My chakras are balanced, clear, and energized. I feel the essence of this perfect vibration flowing through me now. I love this moment. I feel it deep down in my soul.

I intend to spend ten minutes in silence and gratitude this morning and evening for the feeling of this perfect vibration of harmonic balance occurring within me. Being in balance keeps my immune system healthy, my mind sharp, my heart loving, and my communication clear and compassionate.

Day 199

I am a prosperity magnet. Prosperity flows into my life easily and abundantly.

I intend to focus on all that I have in my life. I will see only the energy of abundance and prosperity as I go through my day. I know that this will help to keep me in the constant state of magnetizing, attracting, and manifesting.

Day 200

I am alert, balanced, and calm.

I intend to stay balanced, alert, and calm.

Day 201

I am beautiful in every way. I radiate beauty to all I encounter. I see beauty in my neighborhood, my city, my state, and my world.

I intend to spend time walking through an art museum, a park, or library admiring the beauty and the gift of the creations. I take time to notice the natural beauty all around me. By admiring all types of beauty, I replenish the energy of beauty within me.

Day 202

My life is full of amazing opportunities that are ready for me to step into. This fuels the fire within me, and I am ready leap.

I intend to take a specific action step toward one of the opportunities that are happening in my life now. By taking action, I tell the universe that I am serious and ready for more.

Day 203

I focus on what I need instead of what I want. I appreciate the fact that I am gaining wisdom by doing this.

I intend to take a few minutes to create a list of needs and wants. This will help me to gain perspective of what I truly need versus what I want for self-gratification but does not add or enhance my wellness, wisdom, or wealth.

I release all fear. I release all worry, and I embrace "unstoppability."

I intend to take one courageous act toward turning my passion into purpose or profit. This action will be measurable, beneficial, and opportunity enhancing.

Day 205

I let go of the need to control things beyond my control. This is freeing, grounding, and lightening. This relieves me of any unnecessary excess baggage.

I intend to relinquish my need to control my life and the lives of others to the Divine source. This relieves my mind and body of all unnecessary stress. And I feel great!

Day 206

I imagine my wildest dream happening in real time and with vivid detail. I absorb the energy and emotions of this and process. I welcome my wildest dreams into my life.

I intend to identify one step that I can take that will move me closer to my wildest dreams. I take action and complete that step with commitment, determination, and drive.

Day 207

I embrace the time that I am given to relax, rejuvenate, and recharge. I am grateful and it is reflective in my mind, body, and emotional well-being.

I intend to spend time relaxing in a steam room or sauna by allowing the warm water to relax my muscles and rejuvenate my mind. The time I spend doing this keeps the positive energy circulating in my body and helps to radiate positive vibes in all areas of my life.

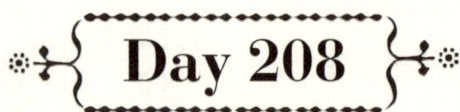

Day 208

There is nothing that can stop me from accomplishing success. My mind accepts this and works to make this happen for me.

I intend to spend eight minutes reflecting on eight successes I've experienced in the last eight days of my life. As I reflect on my success, I allow the emotions associated with how I feel now to become a part of my everyday state of being.

Day 209

I chose not to respond to any negativity today. Instead, I choose to focus and amplify the positivity in my life. I am most powerful when I am positive.

I intend to view all the experiences I encounter in the next twelve hours from a glass half full perspective. This is a key to all things good.

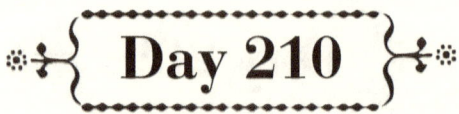

Day 210

I open myself to receive the miracles that are flowing into my life. I trust that all that I am working toward will be successfully accomplished.

I intend to spend twenty-five minutes in solitude and quietness so I can focus on recognizing the miracles occurring in my life.

I know that I am a unique individual; there is no one in this universe like me. I am truly one of a kind.

I intend to give myself pats on the back for recognizing that I am a unique gift to the world. I give gratitude to the Divine for making me a beautiful, unique, and one-of-a-kind person. It feels amazing to know that there is only one me in the universe.

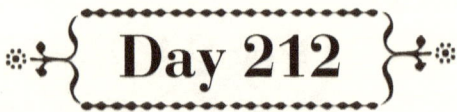

Day 212

I believe that good things are happening in my life right now. I trust that my subconscious mind is always working to make this a reality for me.

I intend to act with faith, knowing that what I desire is magnetizing to me. This act of faith sends a message to the universe that I believe and trust that all that I desire is starting to come into my life. The more I pay attention to the good things, the more the good things show up in my life.

Day 213

I am surrounded by a positive aura that repels all negativity.

I intend to keep my aura clear by smudging myself and the rooms in my home. Smudging is a natural and holistic way to keep my space free of any negative energy and my aura clean and bright.

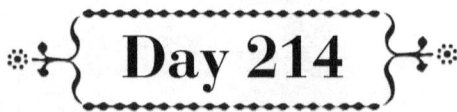

I release all negative thoughts to the universe so that I can be free.

I intend to practice a fifteen-minute guided positive meditation. This assists my mind in releasing the thoughts that are not for my highest benefit and good. A positive meditation practice is freeing, liberating, and healing.

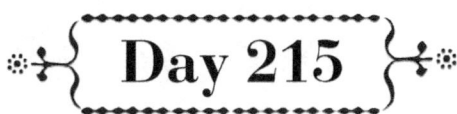

Day 215

I am free to express my wisdom and creativity. I am open to this freedom flowing within me now. I celebrate the freedom to be wise and creative, and it feels good.

I intend to spend time journaling, allowing my hands to write whatever thoughts come into my mind, not caring or thinking about if what I'm writing makes sense. I permit the wisdom of my thoughts to be creatively expressed, and it feels good.

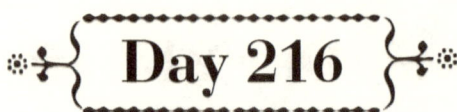

I look around my world today and see all the gifts that the Divine has given to me, and I am very grateful.

I intend to practice an act of gratitude by donating items I no longer need or use to organizations that support women veterans. I give thanks for having the ability to be able to donate to those in need. I know that this is an act of passing good energy and blessings along to others, and I am blessed to be able to do so.

Day 217

I release my judgment of others. I choose to focus on the blessings they are and the important piece of the puzzle they are in this game we call life.

I intend to pay attention to my thoughts, and when I catch myself placing judgment on someone, I stop myself and ask, *Who are you to judge? Without this person appearing in your life, you may have ended up in a completely different situation, which may have not been good.*

A quick reality check is always good for the mind.

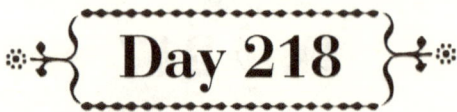

I have a clear head and a calm mind. I am observant and pick up on all the messages being shared with me.

I intend to focus on my sixth chakra by allowing the energy to guide my intuition to highlight what needs my attention. This guidance is divinely given and will always lead to the truth and light of all situations. This information is not ever incorrect. Therefore, I pay attention.

Day 219

I have a positive mental attitude. No matter what is happening in or around me. My mental attitude remains positive.

I intend to set my mental attitude meter to highly positive. I know that when I do this, I amplify the result of more positivity in my life.

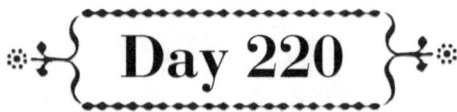

Day 220

In this moment, my body is filled with peace. I am relaxed and serene. The breath I take in rejuvenates my body and my mind.

I intend to practice a breathing meditation such as pranayama, fire breath, water breath, earth breath, cleansing breath, or just focusing on my regular rhythm of breathing for twelve minutes. When I engage in this practice, I benefit from detoxification, relaxation, restoration, and rejuvenation.

Day 221

My body is healthy, well, and functioning at an optimal level. My skin is radiant, glowing, and clear. My muscles are strong, agile, and flexible. I feel amazing!

I intend to spend twenty minutes doing yoga in nature, breathing in the clean air, allowing the sun to naturally produce vitamin D within me, and allowing my muscles the workout that they need to keep me running like a fine-tuned machine.

Day 222

I focus on giving my body what it needs and making sure that I honor it for all that it does for me. I appreciate and love my body.

I intend to spend time doing something that my body loves such as getting a massage, taking a bath, sitting in a hot tub, or taking a long rejuvenating nap. I want my body to know how much I love and appreciate all that it does for me.

Day 223

I am smart and have great recall. I do well on all exams, speeches, or teachings that I engage in.

I intend to spend fifteen minutes reading something new and interesting and ten minutes writing about something that makes me smile. I know that this stimulates my brain cells and helps to keep them active, which is great for recalling bits of needed information.

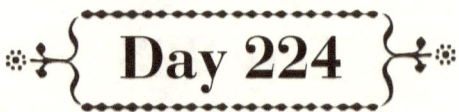

Day 224

I maintain total peace with myself as I continue to grow. I allow peace to fill me from the inside out. The peace within me brings comfort to my growth.

I intend to spend fifteen minutes sitting quietly and in a state of peace. I focus on bring peace to my breathing pattern and relaxing my chest muscles as I breathe. I relax my mind and focus on my breathing. I breathe deeply, completely filling myself with peace.

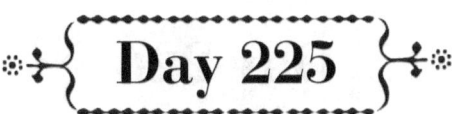

Day 225

My positive mindset attracts positive people into my life.

I intend to keep my thoughts positive. I focus on the positivity that is occurring in my life. I allow this positive energy to fill my body and radiate out of me into the world, magnetizing like-minded people into my life.

Day 226

I am the mastermind behind my destiny.

I intend to spend thirty minutes today writing in my journal what I define as my destiny. I know that to create what I desire, I must have a vision and create a blueprint and map to guide me toward my destiny and all that I desire.

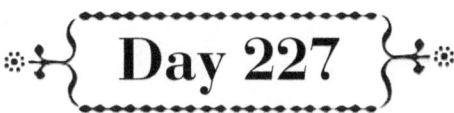

Day 227

I am so confident in my abilities; I cannot be dissuaded.

I intend to take a measurable action step toward a goal that I desire for the next thirty days. Thirty days of action will result in me being thirty times closer to that which I desire, and that feels amazing.

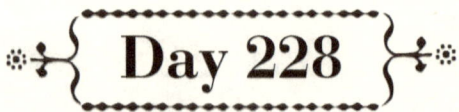

Day 228

I appreciate all my strengths and qualities. I'm so glad that I act on my ideas quickly and efficiently.

I intend to spend ten minutes making a list of my strengths and qualities. At the end of this time, I will read my strengths, qualities, and ideas, gaining insight into how intelligent I am.

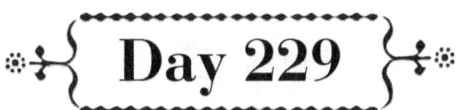

Day 229

My future is deeply rooted in positive experiences. Those who encounter me walk away with an enlightened perspective. I am honored to share my positive energy with the world.

I intend to spend time walking on the grass without shoes or socks, allowing my feet to connect with the earth. I will spend three minutes standing in nature, connecting with earth and grounding, connecting, and rooting myself to the positive energy of Mother Earth.

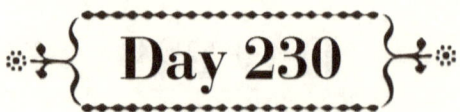

Day 230

Success comes to me as naturally as the air I breathe.

I intend to practice pranayama breathing for ten minutes in the morning prior to starting the day and ten minutes in the evening prior to going to sleep. As I practice pranayama, I focus on breathing in the energy of success and breathing out the energy of success.

Day 231

I am living a custom-made destiny designed by me. I have the power to change any aspect of the destiny that I have designed to keep all in alignment with the direction of my destined, designed journey.

I intend to examine what I envision as my destiny. During this time of destiny examination and reflection, I may discover that what I see as a current purpose may not be the purpose of my future.

Day 232

Self-confidence oozes out of my pores. I am unstoppable. As success is continuously attracted to me, I remain humble in my words and actions. I am confident yet moderate as I pursue my dreams.

I intend to spend time in gratitude for the amazing individual that I am. I love myself and my life. In doing so, I give thanks for the beautiful creation that I am and for the gifts that I must share with the world.

Day 233

My mind is my own personal secret weapon. I use it to create a phenomenal existence.

I intend to meditate in nature about the beauty of nature for fifteen minutes prior to starting the day. The gift of nature has so much information to share with humans. By taking time to become one with nature, the wisdom of existing in a harmonious way is experienced and clarity fills the mind.

Day 234

I make calculated moves toward my goals. My goals consistently restore my zest for the outside world. This enhances the energy around my goals, making them more attracted to me.

I intend to write down one goal that I will act on for the next seven days. By the end of the seven days, I will have accomplished the goal or be well on my way to accomplishing the goal.

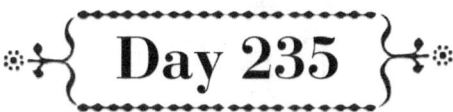

Day 235

I have the courage and strength to become the driving force in my life. Every day, my personal power grows. As my personal power grows, I get more comfortable and confident with the driving force of my life.

I intend to do something that I have never done and that makes me a little nervous and uncomfortable. I use this experience to exercise the muscle of courage and reach for the strength that I have within. It is always good to exercise these muscles to keep them active, energized, and ready to perform, especially when being fearless and strong is required.

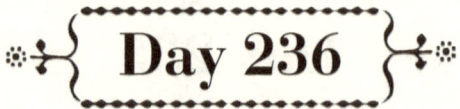

Day 236

I am a vessel for peace, positivity, and love. I remember this as I go about my day. The more I focus on being a vessel for peace, positivity, and love, the more of this energy I send out to the world.

I intend to spend five minutes out of the next eight hours sending loving and peaceful thoughts and energy to the world. As I send out this energy of peace, I replenish the peaceful energy within me. This creates a continuous cycle of peace between the world and me.

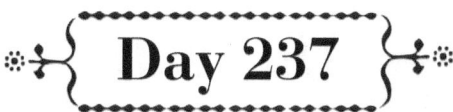

Day 237

I am dedicated to success in my daily life. I continue to take action to make my thoughts more positive, my emotions more joyous, and my intentions more conscious and clearer.

I intend to make time to enjoy the things in life that bring joy to my heart such as eating an ice cream cone, walking barefoot on the grass, laughing until my belly feels like it is going to burst, or spending time with those I love. Being joyful is a recipe for success.

Day 238

I live with passion, purpose, peace, and positivity.

I intend to write down all that I am passionate about, what I believe to be my purpose, all that brings me peace, and how my body feels when I am surrounded by and filled with positivity.

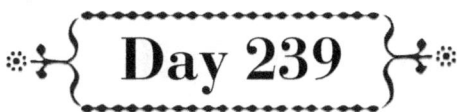

Day 239

I am a valuable being. Within me lies the answers to all my questions. Every aspect of my existence illuminates the definition of success. I am a success.

I intend to spend fifteen minutes writing down all my accomplishments up until this moment in time, being careful to review all aspects of my life. Once I'm done writing, I will read what I have written out loud and with a smile upon my face.

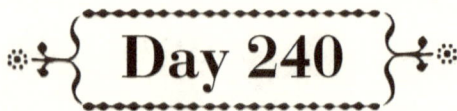

Day 240

I move forward knowing that I am one step closer to achieving my goals. Unfiltered confidence sustains each of my steps. I express pure passion and enthusiasm in pursuing my goals.

I intend to take the next step forward toward pursuing my most immediate goal. This step forward will result in action being taken that is measurable and brings me even closer to my goal. The forward action creates a propelling energy that moves me closer to my goal faster.

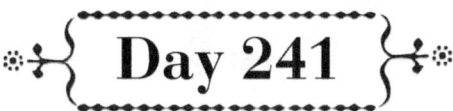

Day 241

I can alter negative thoughts at will, eradicating them from my belief system. I view difficult situations as a challenge. I will not back down. When faced with opposition, I grow even stronger.

I intend to be mindful of the thoughts that occupy my mind. When I notice a negative thought, I immediately rephrase the thought to a positive. I waste no time in rephrasing the thought. I acknowledge the thought, rephrase it, and move on. I repeat this as often as necessary.

Day 242

Waves of abundance are constantly flowing to me. I am deserving of abundance, wealth, and real happiness. I am grateful for the abundance in my life.

I intend to spend time looking at how much money I spend each week and how much money I save each week. If my weekly expenditures are more than the amount I am saving, I will take action to reverse it. I will begin saving more than I spend by creating an automatic flow of cash from my checking account to my savings account every week.

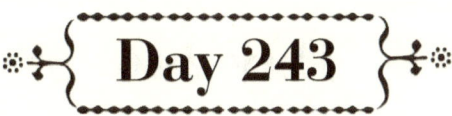

Day 243

Everything I visualize will be achieved in perfect timing.

I intend to spend fifteen minutes visualizing what I desire in my life. I add as much detail as possible to this visualization. As I visualize, I connect to the emotion of how it feels to have what I am visualizing. I internalize this feeling into my body for vibrational memory.

Day 244

I get excited when I think about my potential. Each of my actions are guided by my life's purpose.

I intend to do something that excites me, makes my blood pump, and forces me to stretch beyond the belief of what I envision as my potential. Stretching beyond the limits of my perceived potential allows me to grow, to become stronger and excited.

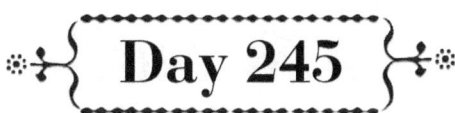

Day 245

I trust the Divine guidance being bestowed upon me now. I use this guidance to manifest the best in my life. I know that Divine guidance will lead me to exactly what is perfect for me right now.

I intend to trust, act with faith, and understand that everything happens for a reason and is always for my highest and best good.

Day 246

I enjoy collaborating with others so that we may create something remarkable from all our strongest qualities. Unification is the key to great change.

I intend to attend a social or networking event with the intention of meeting someone that I can collaborate with. Expanding my sphere of influence is one of the best ways to meet and interact with people with whom I may find a collaborative relationship.

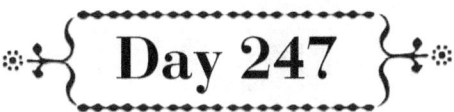

Day 247

My life knows no limits. I live without boundaries. I am a courageous vessel blazing through life's obstacles with ease.

I intend to spend twenty minutes imagining living a life without boundaries, obstacles, or limitations. I tap into the state of feeling free and uninhibited. I know the universe is filled with unlimited possibilities.

Day 248

I assess my decisions by how happy they make me. If it feels good, I charge full steam forward.

I intend to tap into how I feel when confronted with making a decision. Exercising this muscle gives me the ability to become efficient at making correct decisions for me.

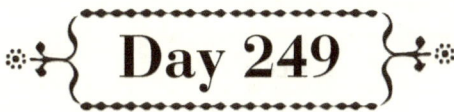

Day 249

I exercise honesty and integrity in all my deeds. I am certain that all my experiences are contributing to my personal development. I trust the process I must take to achieve my goals.

I intend to continue being honest and acting with integrity in all my deeds. I know that by doing this, I honor myself and those that I meet.

Day 250

I am in tune with the frequency of my body. I pay attention to the subtle signals of my body and make the necessary adjustments to keep my body balanced and healthy.

I intend to spend time looking at my body and tuning into how my body feels inside. If I notice that there appears to be an imbalance, I make the necessary adjustments to restore my balance within.

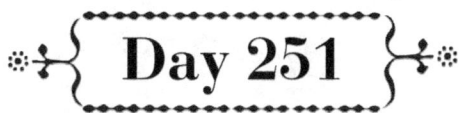

Day 251

I appreciate the resilience and strength of my body. My body is healthy and strong. My mind is healthy and strong, and together they form a powerful bond within me.

I intend to participate in some form of strength training, allowing my muscles to stretch and contract, gaining strength, resilience, and power. This will aid in keeping me agile, flexible, and strong.

Day 252

My business transactions are filled with the genuine qualities of being a win-win situation for all involved. All parties agree, and business is solidified in harmony.

I intend to make sure that all transaction I have are beneficial to all involved.

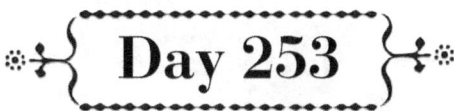

Day 253

I make the right decisions that help me to propel forward on my path to bliss. This includes being at the right place at the right time. Synchronicity is the flow of the day.

I intend to relax in the comfort of knowing that wherever I am, I am in the right place at the right time. All is good and meant to be. I am exactly where I am supposed to be.

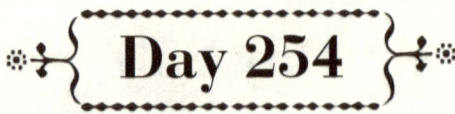

Day 254

The world is a beautiful place. I see beauty in everything. I recognize the beauty in nature and all of life. It feels amazing.

I intend to spend time in a beautiful setting outdoors. Just sitting, observing nature, and spending time in appreciation for the beauty in my life.

Day 255

Wherever I want to go, whatever I want to do, whoever I want to be, I have the power to make it happen, and it begins *now*.

I intend to place my attention on the here and now. When my mind begins to wander, I will refresh it by thinking of the words here and now.

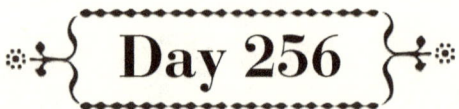

Day 256

Moving my body every day allows my natural energy and frequency to circulate, which allows harmony within the energy centers of my body and mind. The movement keeps me healthy and flexible.

I intend to take a twenty-five-minute walk in nature. Walking is beneficial to the mind, body, and spirit. It allows the mind to refresh, the body to reenergize, and the soul to be released. All helps to keep the immune system strong.

Day 257

Health is within me, around me, and in front of me. I move forward down my path to bliss with visions of a healthy, radiant, and energized me.

I intend to refrain from overeating, hurried eating, or not eating at all. I will choose to refuel my body with healthy and nourishing food that naturally energizes the body and improves the immune system.

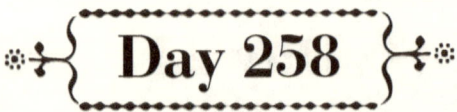

Day 258

My body is flexible, my mind is flexible, and my learning capacity is flexible. I expand and contract as I need to, which allows me to be flexible.

I intend to participate in a form of exercise that allows my body to expand and contact such a yoga, tai chi, or Pilates. Flexibility is a key ingredient to aging gracefully.

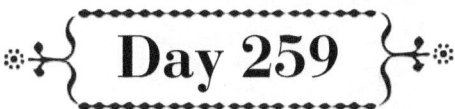

Day 259

My heart is filled with goodness, my mind is filled with love, my spirit is balanced, and I am at peace.

I intend to keep my thoughts centered on the words love, goodness, balance, and peace. These are high-energy words and help to keep my thoughts in an energized and high vibratory state.

Day 260

This is a new day and a new beginning. I take this new opportunity to create something amazing, beautiful, and unforgettable. I am grateful for this new day.

I intend to make this the best day ever because I get another chance to make it as I want it to be. Each new opportunity allows us another shot at being great. I don't take this lightly because I know that each day is a precious moment in time.

Day 261

The wisdom is within me to discover the solution to my cash flow challenges. I believe and know that the highest and best solution is being provided to me now. All I must do is open myself up fully to receive.

I intend to practice the gift of being open to receive. Each time I am confronted with the possibility of receiving, I allow myself to be open to receive. Being in a receiving state of being allows the wisdom that is requested to surface from the depths of the mind and be brought forward for recognition.

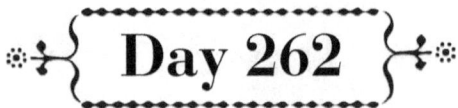

Day 262

I have a healthy and strong body. My body is energized and fit. It provides me all that I need to get through my day with strength, stamina, and vitality.

I intend to spend thirty minutes performing a cardiovascular exercise such as walking outdoors, using the treadmill, elliptical, stair-stepper, or jumping rope. This is good for refueling my body, clearing my mind, and cleansing my soul.

Day 263

I open my heart chakra and focus on giving from my heart. Whatever I give, I energize with love, peace, and positivity.

I intend to concentrate on keeping my heart chakra filled with the energy of the heart chakra colors green or pink. This will keep me in a loving, peaceful, positive state of being. All that I encounter will feel the energy of my heart chakra.

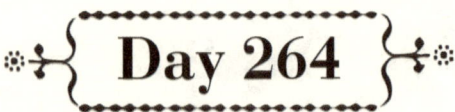

Day 264

Wealth is all around me. I know that my greatest wealth lies in the fact that I am healthy and strong.

I intend to express gratitude to the wealth of my well-being. I know that without well-being, complete wealth is not possible. Well-being is the greatest source of wealth that humans have.

Day 265

I provide my body and mind with the best nourishment available. Doing this helps to keep my immune system functioning optimally and my body free of illness and disease.

I intend to eat three servings of organic fruits and three servings of organic vegetables. The healthier the food choices I incorporate into my daily intake, the better my body feels and operates and the more clarity and peace I experience in my mind.

Day 266

The principles of right action and Divine harmony govern my entire life. I believe and know this to be true.

I intend to take action to ensure that I stay in harmony with the Divine energy circulating in my life. Before I take action, I will ask myself if this flows with the Divine harmony in my life now. The immediate sense I feel after asking this question will tell me if I am in harmony with the Divine energy or if I need to work on being in harmony with the Divine energy prior to me taking the action.

Day 267

I accept the fact that I don't know it all and that I am on a journey of learning and enlightenment. I am OK with this because I know that each step I take forward is an opportunity to do and be better.

I intend to take steps forward on my journey in life with the knowledge that I do not have to know where I am headed. I just need to keep moving forward and enjoy the journey.

Day 268

My strength comes from the strength and wisdom of my ancestors. I tap into this energy and allow it to become a part of my essence.

I intend to spend a few moments thanking my ancestors for the strength that they have given me. I revel in these moments of connection. I know that I am here because of my ancestor's strength, and I am filled with gratitude.

Day 269

My purpose is always being revealed to me. When I get quiet and relaxed, I can tap into this Divine information. The key is to allow myself to get quiet and relaxed.

I intend to spend five minutes in the morning before I get out of bed focusing on my breath and tapping into the Divine information that is being gifted to me. I will repeat this process in the evening prior to going to sleep to allow the information to flow into me as I drift off to a restful sleep.

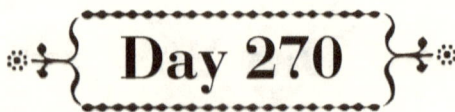

Day 270

My dreams are an everyday reality. The more I realize this, the stronger the energy of my dreams becomes. Through this I can magnetize, attract, and manifest my dreams.

I intend to illuminate the energy of my dreams within me by spending two minutes each waking hour acknowledging all the blessings in my life. By doing this, I add more powerful, magnetizing, and abundant energy to my reality, and it feels amazing.

Day 271

I send out the energy of strength and courage to all that I encounter. The more strength and courage I send out to the world, the stronger and braver I become.

I intend to open my solar plexus chakra and allow the beautiful, loving, and transformative energy of the solar plexus chakra to encompass my entire body. This provides me with a sense of being connected to those I encounter. With the feeling of connectedness, there is no separation.

Day 272

I take time today to appreciate the beauty of nature. Each day is followed by each night. When I wake up, I hear the birds sing. When I step outside, I feel the warmth of the sun on my skin. And I stop to think, *Amazing*!

I intend to spend twenty minutes sitting outside in the sun to naturally replenish my stores of vitamin D, to breathe in fresh, clean air, and to watch the beauty of nature in harmony. This is healing to my mind, body, and soul.

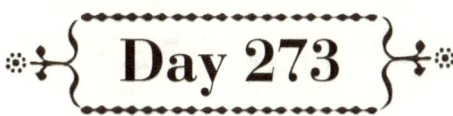

Day 273

The magic of the day begins right now. I will allow my day to naturally unfold and make sure to appreciate every moment.

I intend to stay grounded in the here and now. I anchor my roots in the ground as deep as an oak tree so that I can withstand the push and pull and stay in the present moment. I stay grounded in the here and now. The here and now is the only place that I have control, and I love it.

Day 274

I see my body as beautiful, healthy, radiant, and vibrant. I love my body, and my body loves me back. I am grateful for my beautiful, healthy, radiant, and vibrant body.

I intend to spend two minutes looking at my face and my body in the mirror. I start with the top of my head, appreciating every aspect of it, then I move to my face, my eyes, my nose, my lips, and my mouth. I continue moving down my body, paying close attention to the unique aspects of me. When I get to my feet, I give thanks to my feet for carrying me this far on my journey. I give thanks to my entire essence for the unique gift I am to the world.

Day 275

I give my love freely for the joy and beauty of sharing my love. I radiate love to every living thing. I feel grateful to be able to share my love with the world this way.

I intend to open my heart chakra channel to allow loving energy to flow freely throughout my body, mind, spirit, and all I encounter on this day. The opening of my heart chakra allows the true loving energy within me to flow effortlessly into the world.

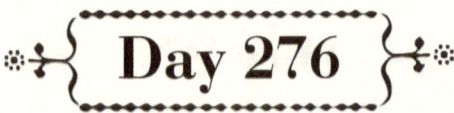

Day 276

I am magnetizing all that I want in my life. I imagine and visualize what I want coming to me in beautiful streams of energy. I am open to receive.

I intend to dedicate fifteen minutes during the day to imagine what I yearn to have in my life. During this imagination time, I grant my mind the freedom to let my imagination run wild. As I do this, I add vivid details with my imagination, bringing specifics to the forefront of my mind. This fuels the energy to magnetize what I long for in my life.

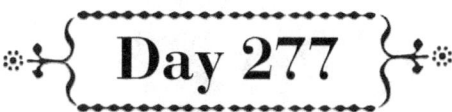

I think, speak, and act lovingly, peacefully, and positively. I radiate love, peace, tolerance, and kindness to all that I encounter. I anchor my thoughts to peace, harmony, and goodwill to all.

I intend not to watch any television or spend any time on social media today. I've decided to utilize my energy on tasks that enhance the peace within me, which allows me to stay focused on the positive and brings goodwill to all.

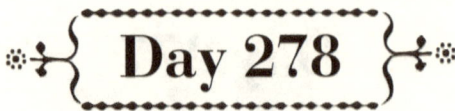

Day 278

I celebrate my amazing growth. I have come a long way. I am blossoming into the beautiful being that I've always imagined. I am grateful for this journey.

I intend to celebrate the growth that I've experienced in my life. I have accomplished many successes, and I continue to reach my goals. Appreciating and celebrating my growth is exactly what I need to be doing right now. And it feels *good*!

Day 279

All workings in my business transactions are honest, sincere, cooperative, faithful, and a win-win for all involved. I radiate love, peace, and goodwill in all that I do with my business and business transactions.

I intend to evaluate the process I operate my business in. I look for areas where the company can improve with creating win-win situations for all employees and customers. I understand that professionalism and quality customer service begin at the top.

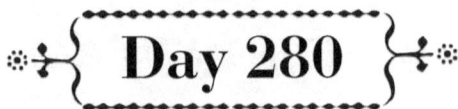

Day 280

When it comes to doing business with my business associates, peace and harmony reign supreme in my mind and body. There is the only correct action in our relationship and business interactions.

I intend to telephone my top customers to thank them for their business and to perform a brief quality assessment on our service with them. I look to keep the conversation open, engaged, and honest with the utmost concern for the customer's satisfaction. Peace and harmony are a key to longevity in life and business.

Day 281

I send the messengers of peace, love, harmony, and goodwill before me when heading to all business activities. Having Divine assistance is always Divine.

I intend to send gratitude for the energy of peace, love, and harmony in my life and I thank the messengers of peace, love, harmony, and goodwill on this day.

Day 282

I go forth into this day full of faith, confidence, peace, trust, and "unstoppability."

I intend to not let anything stop me for doing what I know I am here to do. I intend to meditate for ten minutes about the meaning of the word unstoppable so that I can tap into my unstoppable energy. I am brave, bold, and unstoppable.

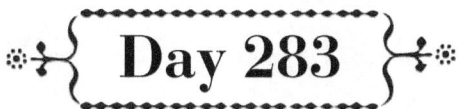

Day 283

I use my words to heal, bless, elevate, inspire, and motivate. I surround myself with universal love and allow the words I speak to fill the room with loving energy.

I intend to pause and think before I speak. I internally ask myself, *Is it the truth, is it helpful, is it inspiring, is it necessary, and is it kind?* And then I proceed. This allows me to stay true to what I affirm.

Day 284

I am relaxed, I am poised, and I am serene. All the work that I am putting in has prepared me for this moment right now.

I intend to celebrate my current state by getting a massage, doing yoga, or practicing some form of physical activity. I know that this is healing to my body and my mind, allowing grace and serenity to relax my soul.

Day 285

Action is a consequence of thought. I know what needs to be done, and I do it in a timely manner. I am organized, efficient, and productive. I prioritize my tasks and perform them in their order of importance.

I intend to create a plan for effectively completing my priorities. I take one measurable action step toward the completion of my number one priority. Taking action leads to more action being taken.

Day 286

I eagerly tackle the most difficult tasks. I have all the knowledge, skills, and resources required to complete all my projects and the perseverance to overcome all obstacles.

I intend to complete the most difficult task that I have today first. As I step into the energy of completing this task, the energy adds fuel for me to complete the next set of tasks on my list. The energy of completion fuels completion.

Day 287

I proceed forward with courage, strength, confidence, and passion. I persevere to my destiny with the force of an unstoppable warrior, and I embrace all of this.

I intend to recognize and be thankful for the warrior courage, strength, passion, and confidence within me. As I embody the warrior within me, I invigorate my spirit with the grace of my ancestors, and I am pleased.

Day 288

Treating my body right makes me feel amazing!

I intend to allocate time for taking a walk by a body of water such as a lake, creek, stream, river, sea, or ocean. As I do this, I soak in the healing power of all five elements of nature. This is soothing and restorative to my internal being.

Day 289

My mind is full of peace, poise, balance, and clarity. I am not afraid of anything in the past, the present, or the future. I meet every situation with faith, calmness, and confidence.

I intend to focus on staying calm and tranquil in my solar plexus chakra. By focusing on this area, my gut can communicate with my third eye, allowing me to tap into the wisdom and guidance within. If I am off track, I will feel it and be able to make the correction back to peace, poise, balance, and clarity.

Day 290

I am not perfect. I am perfection in the making. I am learning the art of forgiveness, and I am gentle with myself as I learn how to forgive. I forgive myself. I am forgiven.

I intend to practice the art of forgiveness. I start with practicing forgiving myself for my misdeeds. I practice forgiving others that have hurt or betrayed me. I practice forgiving society. I practice forgiving the world.

Day 291

There has been a perfect, harmonious solution. It is finished according to Divine order.

I intend to rejoice in the fact that a perfect and harmonious solution has occurred in my life even though I may not recognize it now. That within itself is according to Divine order. I am grateful.

My dreams, aspirations, ideals, and goals in life are the thoughts and mental pictures held in my subconscious mind. I open the gate to allow these thoughts to flow into my conscious mind.

I intend to extend an invitation to my subconscious mind to connect with my conscious mind to facilitate the transfer of this information. The more real I can make it in my mind, the greater the magnetic force becomes to pull it toward me.

Day 293

Life flows through me like electricity through wire. It is an ageless force that constantly invigorates my mind and my body. I feel radiant, vibrant, and youthful.

I intend to tap into the energy of my youth. I reminisce about a time I was growing up and had no cares in the world. Oh, what I good time that was. I use this to refresh the vibrancy of my youth within me now.

Day 294

I eagerly look forward to all that this day is delivering to me. I welcome opportunities to learn and enjoy the beauty that surrounds me. I am curious to explore the wonders of nature as they reveal themselves to me.

I intend to allow the day to just occur. I will step out of my need to control. I will permit the curiosity of the unexpected to keep myself open and free. This is stress reducing and well-being enhancing.

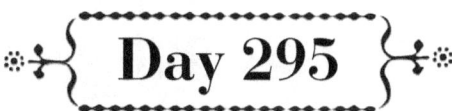

Day 295

My knowledge and experience equip me to overcome challenges that stand between my goals and me. I am energetic, resilient, and have a brilliant mind.

I intend to learn as much as I can about a subject I lack efficient knowledge in. I take the time to locate resources that assist in successfully overcoming the challenges on the road to achieving my goals.

Day 296

I know that no negative thought can ever take root in my mind unless I emotionalize the thought and accept it mentally. I am the gate keeper to the thoughts that I let in my mind. I am in control of my thoughts.

I intend to observe my thoughts. When a negative thought surfaces in my mind, I acknowledge the thought. Say the word *stop* out loud. Then I rephrase the thought to a positive. As not to let the thought become rooted in my mind, I waste no time in following the acknowledge-and- reverse process.

Day 297

From this moment forward, I will grant into my mind for mental consumption only those ideas and thoughts that heal, bless, inspire, and strengthen me.

I intend to be mindful of what I permit into my mind by paying close attention to what I watch, how I talk, and who I spend time with. I refrain from accepting ideas and thoughts that do not heal, bless, inspire, or strengthen me or anyone else.

Day 298

What I visualize in my mind, I can make a reality in my life. I visualize my imagined dreams with vivid details, utilizing all my senses to make the dreams as real as possible. This opens a doorway to the realization of my dreams.

I intend give myself the time to let my imagination run wild. To feel the emotions of my imagination in my gut. This is the source to creative action. When I feel the emotions of my imagination, I ignite the energy of my dreams coming to me like a rocket going toward the moon.

Day 299

I understand the importance of eating the best food possible. I focus on consuming four servings of vegetables with my lunch and with my dinner. This is easy to do and metabolism boosting to my digestive system.

I intend to eat a salad with lunch and a salad with dinner. Ensuring each one contains at least three other vegetables in the salad. This will assure that I get four servings of vegetable with my lunch and dinner. My body will love it.

Day 300

I check in with my body to ask it what it needs, what it wants, and what is the best way to deliver to it. I know my body is wise, and I tune in and listen to what it has to say.

I intend to pay attention to the messages that my body gives me through how I feel. I know that if I am feeling a lack of energy, my body is lacking the fuel or the rest it needs to sustain me. Paying attention to my body is key to optimal health and well-being.

Day 301

Enjoying life is what life is all about. I am free, lively, energetic, happy, healthy, glowing, and dynamic. This moment in life is good. I am enjoying this moment immensely.

I intend to be carefree and fancy in my thoughts, behavior, and all that I do. Enveloping the energy of being free fills my body with enthusiasm and joy. This uninhibited feeling is amazingly beautiful and enchanting.

Day 302

I am amazing, I am smart, I am strong, I am healthy, and I am unique. Enough said!

I intend to repeat to myself throughout the day: *I am amazing, I am smart, I am strong, I am healthy, I am unique, and I am unstoppable.* Enough said!

Day 303

The infinite intelligence of my subconscious mind is leading me and guiding me in all my ways. I embrace this fact to be true; I am grateful to have such a wise and intelligent guide.

I intend to pay close attention to how the infinite intelligence is leading me. Does the infinite intelligence speak to my conscious mind, communicate with my body, or bring the wisdom I need to me in other ways? As I pay attention, I learn exactly the mode of communication my infinite intelligence uses to communicate with me.

Day 304

Today is a beautiful day. It is filled with life and is ready for life to happen. I am ready for life to happen, and I take full control of my life to ensure my path to bliss on this beautiful day.

I intend to observe the beauty of the day as it unfolds. I sit with unexpected anticipation knowing that the beauty of this day and my life is perfect and exactly like it is meant to be. There is no better feeling beyond this state of bliss.

Day 305

My heart is strong and dependable. My stomach works effectively and efficiently. My mind is sharp and clear. My body is in a state of holistic well-being, and it feels amazing.

I intend to check in on the status of the balance within my body. I notice if my *dosha* is out of alignment and not in a harmonious and balanced state. I take immediate corrective action to assist my *dosha* with returning to a state of balance as I know this is for the optimal well-being of my body and mind.

Day 306

I love the adventure of life. I understand that all that I experience in life is meant to help me grow and to become wise. I am grateful for the adventures in my life.

I intend to enjoy whatever occurs during this journey around the sun. All that happens is meant to happen. As I experience the intricate aspects of this journey, I gain wisdom that assists me in appreciating the adventures in my life.

Day 307

I am balanced, nourished, relaxed, and rejuvenated. My body is operating in Divine harmony.

I intend to partake in a detox for the day. I will refrain from eating anything that is not in its natural state. I will drink seven to eight glasses of water. I will drink three glasses of vegetable juice. I will not spend any time on social media. Instead, I will spend time outdoors, breathing in fresh air, connecting with Mother Earth, and allowing the sun to naturally restore and nourish my body with natural vitamin D.

Day 308

Beauty, love, peace, and happiness are mine. I know that I am beautiful, peaceful, loving, and happy. I accept this as my eternal truth of life. It feels naturally satisfying.

I intend to relish in the natural beauty within me. I only see the uniquely beautiful, Divine being that I am. I acknowledge the unique gifts of my natural beauty. I am an intricate and necessary part of the universe.

Day 309

I give my love freely to all for the joy and thrill of knowing that all who receive it will be joyous and free. My gift of love has no strings attached. It is a free as the wind.

I intend to be uninhibited by anything that occurs. I stay in the free zone. I flow as the wind flows, undisturbed by barriers, challenges, or encumbrances.

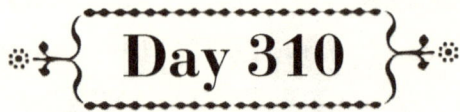

Day 310

I expect nothing of this day except what each moment brings to me. I acknowledge this thought throughout my day. This restores openness and allows me to experience the freedom of expectations.

I intend to go forward without any expectations. I know that expectations are the greatest source of unhappiness. I choose to be happy as I move forward free of expectations. This feels amazing.

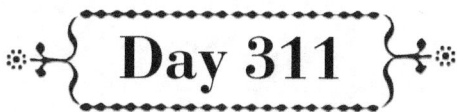

Day 311

I fully and freely forgive those who have hurt me. I release them mentally and spiritually. I completely forgive everything connected with the matter in question. I am free, and they are free. This is an amazing feeling.

I intend to contemplate what it means to truly forgive. I seek to understand so that I can heal all the hurts that are within me. As I do this and go forward on my path, my baggage gets a little bit lighter and my journey becomes a little bit easier.

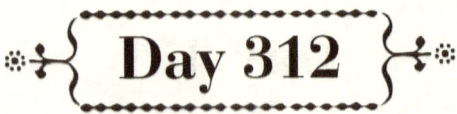

Day 312

I focus on what I want, and I go after it. I know that when I focus, my goals become clear, the strategies to achieve them become more defined, and my visions of success turn into feelings of success.

I intend to be laser sharp when identifying the strategies that will assist me with accomplishing my goals. I focus on one strategy at a time, knowing that this will keep me headed in the direction of accomplishment and success.

Day 313

It is my day of general amnesty. I release anyone and everyone's energy that does not belong to me or is not a match to mine. I send back to them their energy with love, peace, and joy.

I intend to do a twenty-minute release meditation. During my meditation, I focus on the word release. I visualize all that is within me that does not belong to me being cleansed from me and released back to where it belongs.

The practice of releasing is good and healing for the mind, body, and spirit.

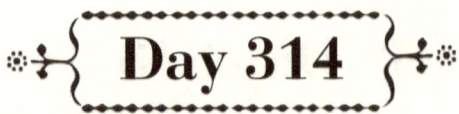

Day 314

My subconscious mind knows what is best for me. I honor and value my subconscious mind. I believe my subconscious mind always leads me to my highest and best good. I am honored to be connected to my subconscious mind.

I intend to thank my subconscious mind for always having my back. Even when I am not aware, my subconscious mind is focused on the principles of right action and Divine order that are appropriate for me. My subconscious mind will not ever lead me astray.

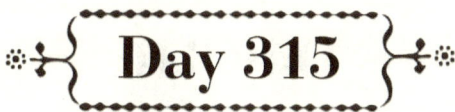

Day 315

I know that my subconscious mind is revealing to me the answer I now seek. I open my heart center, slow my breathing, calm my mind, and wait for the answer to come. The answer I seek is in this space.

I intend to spend some time in quiet and solitude. I will remove myself from the action of life happening around me for just a few moments so that I can get quiet to listen for the answers to my questions from within. I know that in order to hear the answers I seek, I must quiet my mind and my space. In this place is where the answers reside.

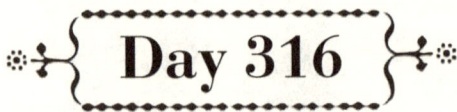

Day 316

My sleep is restorative, rejuvenating, peaceful, healing, and balancing. I sleep through the night and wake up revitalized and refreshed.

I intend to take time to prepare my bedroom for a beautiful night's sleep by turning off all blue light devices thirty minutes prior to retiring for the night or remove all blue light devices from my sleeping area. By doing this, I remove the distractions that hinder my natural rhythm of sleep.

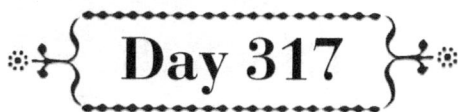

Day 317

My digestive system is operating at an optimal level. My body metabolizes all the nourishment I take in effectively and efficiently. I am an energized, healthy, radiant human being. This feels *fabulous*!

I intend to keep my digestive fire operating in a harmonious state by eating the foods that are nourishing and balancing to my *dosha*. By making the correct food choices for my *dosha*, I keep my digestive fire balanced, which helps with the removal of toxins from my body and keeps my weight in check.

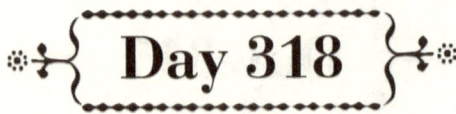

Day 318

My health and well-being are my greatest assets. I listen to my body and give it what it needs to stay healthy and well. I make my health and well-being the number one priority in my life.

I intend today to schedule all my upcoming yearly examinations with my doctor and my dentist. I take note of anything that I want to discuss during my examination. I know that being honest about my state of well-being with my healthcare provider is important to manage my well-being.

Day 319

I am a money magnet. Money is a source of energy. The universe is filled with the energy of money. There is an abundant supply of money energy in the universe. I feel this abundant energy of money flowing to me now.

I intend to pay attention to how I feel when I am in the process of spending money. I will observe if I am filled with abundant, positive energy or lacking, fearful energy. This information will tell me if I am magnetizing money to me or if I am repelling money from me. This is the key to correcting the course of money energy flowing to me.

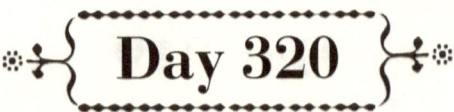

The Divine is the source of my supply of all my needs. The Divine's wealth is circulating in all areas of my life. There is always a Divine surplus. The Divine's supply is never ending. There is more than enough for everyone.

I intend to monitor my thoughts to see if I am thinking from a perspective of lack or a perspective of abundance. When I notice thoughts of lack, I reframe the thoughts by thinking of abundance. I know that even though I may feel lack, the Divine supply is vastly abundant.

Day 321

Every day and every night, I am prospering in all my interests and ways. Everything I am doing is being filled with the energy of prosperity. I am prosperous.

I intend to donate items that are no longer needed or used and that are still in great shape such as clothing, books, shoes, or anything else. This will open space in my heart, in my home, in my life, and in my energy field, creating space for more prosperity to flow into my life.

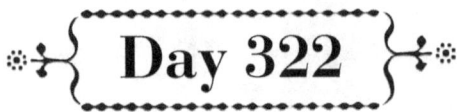

Day 322

Infinite wisdom governs and watches over all my financial transactions. Whatever I sow shall prosper. I see my investments flourishing and my wealth growing.

I intend to look at my bank statements, investment statements, and any other statements of financial assets that I hold with the goal of reviewing trends, gains, and losses. By doing this on a monthly basis, I will be able to keep abreast of where I stand in the prosperity arena and have the knowledge to know when it's time to make adjustments to protect my wealth.

Day 323

This is a new beginning. This is a wonderful new beginning to a wonderful new day. There will never be another day like this one. This is the first day of the rest of my fabulous life.

I intend to treat this day as if I get to start my life afresh. Life is precious and every day is a blessing. Every day is a chance to start over and be the best that you can be, and this is my day.

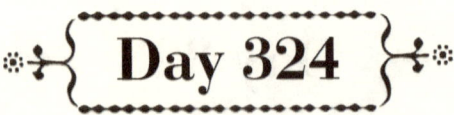

Day 324

Divine love surrounds me, enfolds me, and envelopes me. I go forth with happiness, love, joy, and peace.

I intend to remember that Divine love surrounds me, enfolds me, and envelopes me. This is enough to sustain me. The thought of this fills me with the feeling of Divine love. Oh, what an amazing feeling.

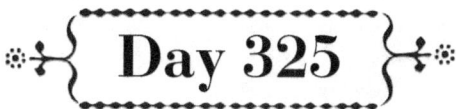

Day 325

I am a spiritual and mental magnet that attracts all things that bless, heal, and prosper.

I intend to invest twenty minutes reflecting on all that I have been blessed with and that has brought healing and prosperity into my life. While reflecting, I tap into the feeling of each blessing and silently give thanks.

Day 326

My toes are relaxed, my ankles are relaxed, my abdominal muscles are relaxed, my heart and lungs are relaxed, my neck is relaxed, my face is relaxed, my eyes are relaxed, and the top of my head is relaxed. My mind and my body are in sync.

I intend to practice the technique of relaxing each part of my body, starting with my toes and working my way up to the top of my head. As I relax each part of my body, I allow my mind to unwind.

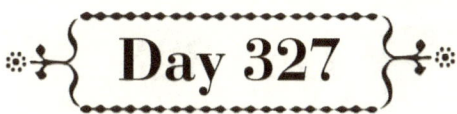

Day 327

I rest in peace and serenity. My mind and my body are calm. My whole being quiets, and I feel the Divine presence within me.

I intend take time quieting my mind and relaxing my body before I settle down to sleep. This is soothing to my soul and accelerates the process of falling into a deep, peaceful, and restful sleep.

I am filled with free-flowing, cleansing, healing, and harmonizing vitality. My body is the temple of my soul. It is pure and perfect in every way.

I intend to pay attention to all that I eat and drink with the intent of eating and drinking substances that are healthy, balancing, and nourishing to my *dosha*. I appreciate the fact that keeping my *dosha* balanced is a key to my well-being.

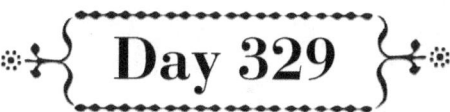

Day 329

I enjoy the present moment and eagerly look forward to my glorious future. I know that Divine timing is working for me. All is in Divine order.

I intend to be present in this exact moment. Nothing is more important than this moment right now. Everything beautiful is in the moment. This moment is unique. There will be no other moment like this Divine moment right now.

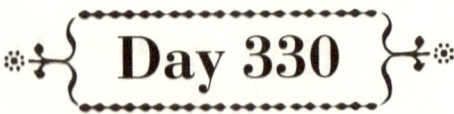

Day 330

I walk through fear to fearlessness. I move from lack to abundance. I see fruitful opportunities all around me. I am brave, bold, and unstoppable. I take action.

I intend to do two things that I have never done in my life. The first thing will include the emotion of bravery. The second thing will include the feeling of abundance. Together the two will exhibit the qualities of being brave, bold, and unstoppable. It's OK to step out of the box and be creative.

Day 331

My true place in life is being revealed to me. My interest, knowledge, talents, skills and passions are being brought together in harmony. I understand this revelation. I open to the flow of the perfect opportunities surfacing in my life.

I intend to sit and contemplate this affirmation, allowing it to reverberate throughout my mind and body. I pay close attention to what is showing up in my life, knowing that I am being provided clues and information to assist me on my journey.

Day 332

Life is a gift. I am a gift of life. All living species are a gift of life. The universe is a gift. We are all connected. We are all *one*.

I intend to spend eight minutes writing down whatever thoughts come to mind while I read this affirmation out loud. I write freely and without passing judgment as the thoughts flow into my mind. At the end of the writing session, I read what I have written. This will give me insight to my present state of thinking regarding the gift of life.

Day 333

I am compensated well for my valuable innovations, my creative ideas, my processes, and my products and services. I enjoy what I do. It feels good to be valued and appreciated.

I intend to give thanks for the compensation I receive for the gifts I have to offer. I openly accept the compensation. I know that valuing myself and what I have to offer is the most important gift that I can give myself.

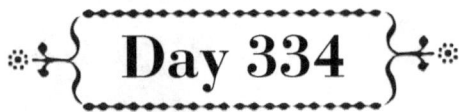

Day 334

Life flows through me like electricity. It is an ageless force that constantly invigorates my mind and body.

I intend to give the best that I can in all that I do. It is my belief that when I do the best that I can, I honor and respect the person I am meant to be. This stimulates the life force energy within me and strengthens the connection to my soul.

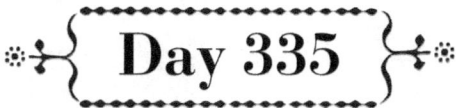

Day 335

New opportunities are presenting themselves to me. I am curious to explore the wonders of these opportunities as they appear in my reality. I attract opportunities that help me achieve my goals.

I intend to pay close attention to the details of the opportunities streaming to me. I have faith that what I need will present itself to me through the opportunities that are popping into my life.

My knowledge and experience have equipped me to handle anything that comes my way. I overcome all challenges that stand between me and my goals. I am vigilant, resilient, and immortal.

I intend to access the resources within my mind to assist me with handling any difficulties that appear on my journey. I am a wealth of information and have an abundance of experience.

Day 337

I put out into the world what I want in return. My world is a mirror of my thoughts. My thoughts are good, therefore, my world is good.

I intend to think of what I want my world to be and how I want to experience my world. I know that my thoughts create my world, and I have the power to control my thoughts to create my world the way I want it to be.

I welcome prosperity in every aspect of my life. I know that when I am open to receive, prosperity flows into my life. I am the source of my own happiness and prosperity.

I intend to keep the door of prosperity open by exhibiting generosity. I give from my heart without any expectation of receiving. The act of giving makes me happy and warms my soul.

Day 339

The ebb and flow of money is working just fine in my life right now. I have all that I need at any given moment. I acknowledge the goodness of this ebb and flow and am thankful for all that I receive.

I intend to make certain that I do not block the flow of money coming into my life by acting in a selfish and fearful manner. I appreciate what I have, and I recognize when I need to give. This creates synergy and harmony with the pathway for the energy of money.

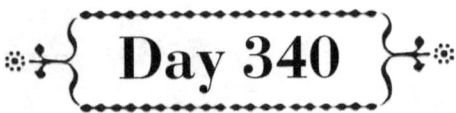

Day 340

I give freely and generously from my heart. I expect nothing in return, and it feels amazing to be free.

I intend to give generously and freely from my heart by surprising someone with a free coffee, meal, or gift card anonymously. The blessing is in the anonymity.

Day 341

My life is filled with prosperity, abundance, and goodwill. Right now, I am creating a fantastic future for myself. I am the source of my own happiness and prosperity.

I intend to spend time doing whatever makes me happy and fills my soul with joy. I laugh, I play, I have fun, and I just enjoy life with the happiest of happy feelings within me.

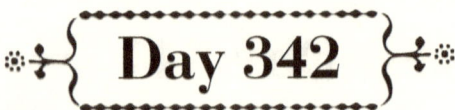

Day 342

I put out into the world what I want in return. I refuse to entertain thoughts of fear and negativity. I know that no negative thought can ever take root in my mind unless I emotionalize the thought and accept it mentally.

I intend to choose thoughts of positivity and fearlessness. I allow the roots of positivity to sprout in my mind and the energy to flow through my body.

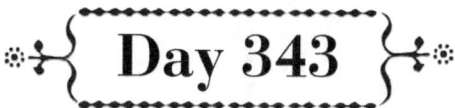

Day 343

My world is a mirror of my thoughts. I see endless successful opportunities before me. Success follows me everywhere I go. I firmly believe in my ability to attract success.

I intend to proceed forward with the successful opportunity that has presented itself to me. Being proactive will allow this opportunity to become a reality.

Day 344

I am releasing all insecurities and growing more comfortable in my own skin. My body is beautiful and appealing. My body is the greatest gift.

I intend to make a bold statement with my fashion choice for the day. I dress with flare, pizazz, and confidence. I display confidence, beauty, and enticing energy.

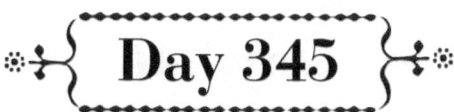

Day 345

My health and well-being are improving each day. I take action to keep my body active. I move it to the beat of my own drum and the rhythm of my own flow.

I intend to dance with the rhythm of my life. I tap into these vibrations and give them permission to become one with me. I let my body pulsate to the tempo of the beat of my life. This keeps me active and gleaming.

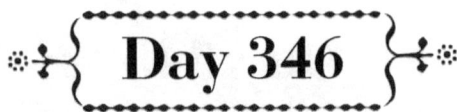
Day 346

Health is mine. Peace is mine. Wealth is mine. Success is mine. I claim it now.

I intend to do something that makes me happy, brings peace to my mind, adds to my state of wealth, and allows me to see all the success that I have achieved. I recognize, appreciate, and value all that I am.

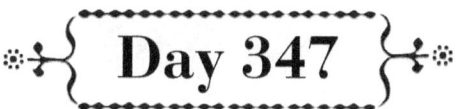

Day 347

I love my feet. My feet are reliable, strong, and healthy. I am grateful for the burden they carry. I love my strong and healthy feet.

I intend to get a foot massage, reflexology, or any spa treatment that incorporates taking care of my feet. This is grounding, relaxing, soothing, and restorative to the muscles and supportive structures in my feet.

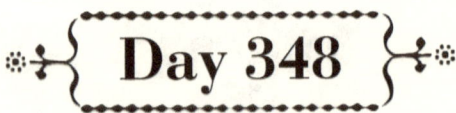

Day 348

My heart is loving and filled with kindness. No matter what is going on in my life or around me, I always remember to tap into the love and kindness that fills my heart.

I intend to tell the loved ones in my life that I love them. I concentrate on sharing love and kindness to all I encounter on my journey on this day. This is good for me and good for the world.

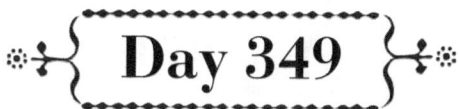

Day 349

I am the master of my thoughts. There is nothing to fear. I imagine myself in the presence of strong souls. I tap into their essence. Their fearlessness and strength are with me always.

I intend to direct my thoughts to those of being fierce and fearless. I am surrounded by the light of Divine beings. It is through this light that I find the courage and strength to go forward without fear.

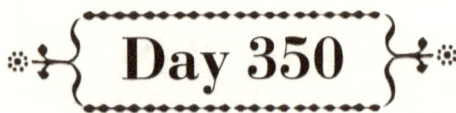

Day 350

The Divine is the source of my wisdom. This wisdom is supplied to me now. The Divine's riches flow to me freely, copiously, and abundantly. I am conscious of the abundant and never-ending supply of wisdom. I openly receive.

I intend to meditate with a clear, open mind and an open heart. By doing this, I free myself from being inhibited by thoughts and feelings and allow the wisdom of the Divine to flow into me. I understand that the universal supply is all-wise and that wisdom is in unlimited supply through the Divine.

Day 351

I act with confidence and have a plan. I accept that plans change. I am adaptable to change. I am supported by my plans.

I intend to review my current plan. I adjust my plan to keep it in line with my current goals. I am confident that the modifications to my plan will keep me on track as I journey toward my current destination.

Day 352

I live a focused and balanced life. I focus on balancing all the aspects of my life. I focus on being the best that I can be. With balance and focus, I can achieve anything.

I intend to focus on maintaining a balanced life. I identify the aspects of my life that cause imbalance, and I create an action plan to restore balance to those areas of my life. Balance keeps my mind, body, and spirit in harmony.

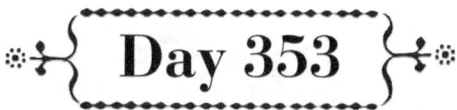

Day 353

I visualize my dreams with vivid detail. The more detail I add to my visualizations, the more real my dreams appear to be. The vivid details of my dreams are easily accepted by my subconscious mind.

I intend to fill my subconscious mind with the vivid details of my dreams. I take the time to write down the vivid details of my dreams. I spend fifteen minutes prior to going to sleep meditating and visualizing the details of my dreams. I know that doing this helps manifest my dreams in reality.

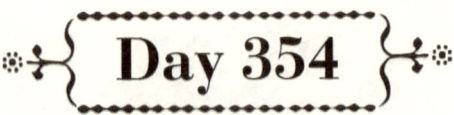

Day 354

I am relaxed and peaceful because I trust in the process of life. I know inner peace is possible. I am surrounded by peace.

I intend to use the word peace to keep myself in a peaceful state of being. I will spend five minutes breathing in peace and breathing out stress. This allows calmness to wash over me, and this feels amazing and nourishing to all parts of my body.

Day 355

I believe that it is OK to practice humility. I practice being humble. I trust that learning to be humble is part of my journey.

I intend to practice humility. I accept this assignment of being humble. My thoughts are focused on humility. I recognize the need to be humble in my life. And I know that it is OK to be a humble individual.

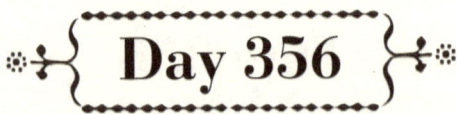

Day 356

I am an island of calm in a sea of uncertainty. I am the calm in the chaos. When the craziness of life around me creates havoc in my own, I choose to face it with calmness.

I intend to practice the art of being calm. Being in a calm state of being helps me to remain poised when challenged by the busyness of life. This is a powerful place to be.

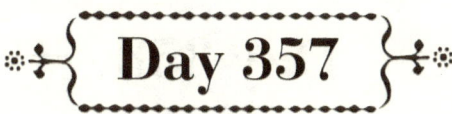

Day 357

I thank the Divine for every new day I am given. I know the Divine is always watching over me. I am loved and cherished by the Divine.

I intend to spend eight minutes in solitude to connect with the energy of the Divine. During this time, I give thanks to the Divine from the energy of my heart. I open myself to receive the loving energy that the Divine replenishes my body and soul with.

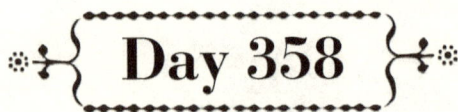

Day 358

My mind is open to receive the wisdom that is being granted to me. I use this wisdom to better myself in all that I do.

I intend to allow the wisdom of the Divine to guide me in all that I do. I take time to stop and think before I respond to any challenges that come my way. This allows me to act based on wisdom versus impulse.

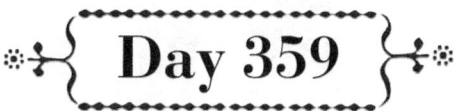

Day 359

Money comes to me in miraculous ways. Financial doors are opening for me. I am excited that I attract money into my life right now. I radiate abundance.

I intend to take stock on all the ways that money is flowing into my life right now. I adjust my finances to ensure that I keep the door of abundance open. I acknowledge the power that this process has over the consistent flow of money in my life.

Day 360

My mind is clear, my body is strong, and my spirit is free. I can achieve whatever I set out to achieve because today is my day.

I intend to act appreciative of my clear mind, strong body, and free spirit. I set out to be the best that I can be. I act with clarity, strength, and the feeling of the being unrestricted as I move toward my goals.

Day 361

I am a prosperity magnet. I attract prosperity. I manifest prosperity. I am prosperous in all my endeavors.

I intend to think about prosperity as being unlimited, vast, free-flowing, and uninhibited and rushing into my life like the ocean crashing upon the shore.

Day 362

When I seek to see goodness in the world, goodness is what I will see. I focus on the goodness within me and the goodness in all those that I encounter. All is good.

I intend to spend twenty minutes writing down all the goodness that has occurred in my life this year. As I recognize the goodness in my life, I open up a portal for more goodness to come into my life.

Day 363

I radiate abundance. I am aligned with the energy of abundance. I am financially abundant, and money comes to me naturally. Every day, in every way, I am becoming more and more abundant.

I intend to spend ten minutes sitting quietly, feeling the energy of abundance that is surrounding my body. As I sit with the energy of abundance, I begin to vibrate the frequency of abundance, and it feels beautiful.

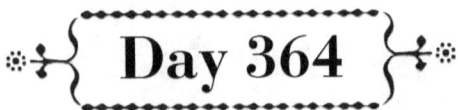
Day 364

I am filled with integrity and light. I trust in the plans that the Divine has for me. Every day brings me greater understanding of the universal force in action.

I intend to spend one minute of each hour of this day in gratitude to the Divine for the blessings in my life. Each time I practice this act of gratitude, I am filled with more love, integrity, and light. This is nourishing to my soul.

Day 365

Wellness, wisdom, and wealth are mine. I am grateful for the blessings flowing into my life right now. I know that all that I seek and desire shall be mine, and Divine timing is perfect. I accept this and go forth with confidence that my dreams, hopes, and aspiration are manifesting now.

I intend to dedicate this day to the Divine light that resides within me. I make choices that are honorable, loving, peaceful, joyful, healthy, and that keep the light of the Divine shinning bright within me. This is the light that speaks to my soul, that guides me through the darkness, and that illuminates the answers I need as I travel down my path to *bliss*.

Next Steps

Commit to affirming, making intentions, and acting as if your life depends on it—in many ways, your life does depend upon it—if you want to experience a life of *bliss*.

As you start using the process detailed in this book, be gentle with yourself and take it easy. Taking it a step further, you'll understand the importance of following the process outlined in the book to make affirmations and intentions an easy and natural part of your day. As you get more comfortable with the process, you'll quickly and easily see sprinklings of bliss showing up in your day and your life.

It's important to note your thoughts create your reality, and the sooner you take back some control of your thoughts—since it's impossible to control all your thoughts, the faster your life will begin to change and align with what you desire. You will begin to live life more intentionally and with a more direct focus versus haphazardly moving through life by using the trial-and-error method.

Just imagine becoming so powerful with affirming what you want in life, taking an intended action, and emitting such powerful energy that even the grandest dreams and desires you have begin to show up in your life faster than you expected and beyond your wildest dreams. This is not a fantasy, my friends; this can become a reality.

Let me be honest, I make no promises that your desires will manifest by using the process outlined in this book. What I do want to say is that if you believe that your thoughts create your reality, if you are tired of living life haphazardly, if you want to feel a bit more control in your life, if you desire to add a bit more energy to magnetize what you desire in life and in business, if you desire an improved feeling of health and well-being of the mind and body, better relationships, more peace, more love, healing or wealth, then I invite you to take this year long journey to begin the transformation of your life.

You deserve to live a life filled with *bliss*.

You deserve to know that it is possible to control a bit of your reality.

You deserve to experience the essence of love, peace, joy, well-being, wisdom, and wealth that the Divine desires you to have.

- See the affirmation,
- Say the affirmation,
- Hear the affirmation,
- Do the affirmation, and
- Have the affirmation!

Let your journey of a year of bliss begin. ☺

Conclusion

365 Days of Affirmations for a Year of Bliss was created from the realization that affirmations have power, and when coupled with intentions, that power increases a thousand times over. Although affirmations may seem like a new age tool, the use of affirmations has existed for centuries.

Using affirmations can change your thoughts. This technique puts you in charge of what and how you think. With the repetitive declarations, you create a habitual way of thinking, which will ultimately begin to show in you and your life.

Taking action is always an essential factor when it comes to having and living a life of bliss. Without action, an affirmation is just a wish. This is where adding an intention to the process becomes an efficient, handy accelerator. The use of intending to act and stating the affirmation throughout the day is a game changer.

When I discovered that adding transformative energy to my affirmation enhanced what I affirm, it opened my mind. It took my affirmation practice to a new level. I watched my affirmations turn into realities in both my business and my life. I had discovered a game changer, however, I wondered why no one talked about this. The more I searched to find out why this information was missing, the more I discovered less about the connection between the two.

That was over thirty years ago, and I have sat on sharing this for all that time. I'm not sure why, however, I know that when the Divine has a purpose for you, Divine timing is always perfect, and you will be guided on how to share the wisdom divinely bestowed upon you.

My desire for this book is for you to enjoy the day-to-day journey of creating a year of bliss and to use the book year after year to create a year of bliss every new year of your life. The gift of having a book like this is that we can share the words of wisdom within it with people we love and can further pass these words on by sharing the book with everyone. The beauty of this book is that it can be shared with teenage kids and adults. What a great gift to share this book with a teenager so that they can get an early start on learning how to create a life of bliss.

Thank you for allowing me your time. Thank you for purchasing, reading, and sharing this book. Thank you for being a part of my journey to assist as many people as possible, like you, to transform their lives so that they can live the life of their dreams.

You now have in your hands a tool to assist you to create a life filled with bliss so that you can start truly having and living the life of your dreams.

Divine timing is one of the greatest gifts bestowed upon us, and when we understand this fact, our lives begin to change for the better. It is Divine timing that you have this book in your hands now. It is Divine timing that you are about to embark on this yearlong journey of bliss. It is Divine timing that I have entered your life, and it is Divine timing that we are now and always connected. I wish you many blessings of bliss in your life.

Namaste.

https://www.blissfulliving4u.com
https://www.unstoppable-womens-summit.com
https://www.facebook.com/rochele.lawson.5
https://www.instagram.com/in/rochelemarielawson
https://www. https://www.youtube.com/@RocheleLawson/streams

Acknowledgments

Each of us has a gift hidden within the discovery of our Divine purpose. There is not a person on this planet who does not have what I like to call our "special power." The magic of our dream life can be discovered in the discovery of this power. I'm honored to have the chance to thank the people who've touched my life and inspired me to be the queen that I am and live the life of bliss that I live.

My thanks to the Divine, my higher power, and my Divine team that guides me on my journey as I travel down my path to bliss, sharing my gift with the world. I could not have done this without you. The guidance and wisdom bestowed upon me from the Divine realm guides me and provides my soul with the nourishment it needs to thrive. It is the fuel that ignites my soul and keeps me transforming, growing, and evolving to be the best I can be.

Heavenly gratitude goes to my grandmother Ethel, who had a class and sophistication about her that I wanted to immolate. It is through my conversations with my grandmother that I learned that there was more to life than what I could see with my eyes and that my life began when I discovered how to enjoy the process of *living* life. The magical conversations we had when I was a little girl have made an impact on much of my life. Thank you for showing me what it means to be classy, sophisticated, caring, independent, successful, and spiritual.

A heartfelt thank you to my children, Khrystopher and Lauryn, who reminded me about the power of using affirmations all those years ago.

The wisdom that comes from the mouth of babes is powerful, especially when they are used as a conduit for sharing wisdom from the Divine.

This project could not have been possible without the assistance of my oldest and dearest childhood friend and editor, Leslie Karen Kinney. She took the time to assist me with the very tedious parts of the project—suggesting edits, correcting sentence structures, and keeping me on task toward completion. I appreciate your grace, suggestions, and insightful wisdom. It is a blessing to have you still in my life after fifty years.

Thank you to everyone that encourages me to share my gift with the world. I appreciate your kind words, support, followings, attendance at my events, purchases of my products and programs, listening and downloading my podcast interviews, and sharing me with your world.

It has been a longtime dream of mine to publish a book with wisdom that has helped me in all areas of my life and in my businesses. And now I get to share my words of wisdom with all of you, which is *fabulous*! Dreams really do come true!

And *you*. Thank you for taking a brave, bold, and unstoppable step toward having and living your dream life. I applaud you for wanting to elevate and transform your life into the life of your dreams—a life filled with daily bliss. You have not only given yourself a life-changing gift but also allowed yourself to change your life year after year to create the life you are meant to live. By taking steps toward living a life filled with bliss, you are creating a wonderful world for yourself and those in your life. You become the gift of life that you were always meant to be. Step in to see it, claim it, be it, have it, and live it. Now is your time.

With sincerity in my heart, *I thank you*.

About the Author

A highly driven woman who was born to break barriers, known as the Queen of Feeling Fabulous, Rochel Marie Lawson is a successful multiple-business owner, RN, AHP, a Dream Lifestyle Transformation facilitator, a multiple best-selling author on Amazon, a two-time international best-selling author, international speaker and creator of The Brave, Bold & Unstoppable Women's Summits™, and owner of Blissful Living 4 U, created to bring wellness, wisdom, and wealth into the lives of individuals ready to unlock, have, and live the life of their dreams.

Rochel Marie proves that when powered by purpose, women are unstoppable. She's built her storied life and career brick by brick, fighting fears, failures, and setbacks to have the success she's always known was hers to claim.

Today she personifies what it means to ascend above adversity while inspiring countless other to do the same. Having honed her expertise over three decades, her work is a testament to what it means to leave an undeniable mark on the world.

She inspires. She empowers. She unleashes.

Extraordinary at walking others through radical transformation, she is as relentless about her clients' success as she is her own. She is more than their coach, she's their champion. She doesn't simply change lives—she expands them.

Rochel Marie Lawson's energy, insight, guidance, and enthusiasm have helped thousands of people improve their wellness, wisdom, and wealth by utilizing ancient holistic principles that unlock the access for transformation to occur. She has been quoted in *Huffington Post* and featured on Fox, CBS, NBC and several other prominent media publication outlets.

https://www.blissfulliving4u.com
https://www.unstoppable-womens-summit.com
Facebook: facebook.com/rochele.lawson.5
LinkedIn: linkedin.com/in/rochelemarielawson
Instagram: instagram.com/rochelelawson/
Instagram: **instagram.com/blissfulliving_4u**
Twitter: **twitter.com/rochelelawson/**
Youtube: https://bit.ly/3KV1tDU

How you can get more of
Rochel Marie Lawson, PhD, RN, AHP, CMS
The Queen of Feeling Fabulous

BLISSFUL LIVING4U

Don't forget to check out *The Blissful Living Podcast* on

Megaphone: https://cms.megaphone.fm/channel/theblissfullivingshow

Youtube: https://www.youtube.com/@RocheleLawson/streams

Spotify: https://open.spotify.com/show/0YtIYl7lohYYkbhK0Pyt8h
?si=aae19bdc7dbb49fa

Castbox: https://castbox.fm/vh/6539432

Amazon Music: https://music.amazon.com/podcasts/7ac90e4c-5c2e-
4066-9287-e0b73f22252d/the-blissful-living-show

iHeart Radio: https://www.iheart.com/podcast/269-the-blissful-liv
ing-show-60471724/

Apple Podcast:https://podcasts.apple.com/us/podcast/blissful-living
-roch%C3%A9le-m-lawson-rn-bsn-ahp-cms/id555679390

Blissful Living Website: https://blissfulliving4u.com/podcast/

Other Best-Selling Books and Collaborative Books
By Rochel Marie Lawson, PhD, RN, AHP, CMS
The Queen of Feeling Fabulous

Intro to Holistic Health Ayurveda Style

The Live Sassy Formula

Rapid Change for the Heart Centered Woman

Answering The Call

The Wellness Universe Guide to Complete Self Care: 25 Tools for Stress

The Wellness Universe Guide to Complete Self Care: 25 Tools for Goddesses

Visionary Women Leaders: Discovering the Greatness Within You

Unstoppable Being Fierce, Fearless and Unf&ckwithable in Life and Business

Love Warriors: The Conscious Expert's Guide to Healing, Joy and Manifestation

The Unstoppable Woman's Manifesto